SCULPTURE
AS
EXPERIENCE

SCULPTURE

ʌS EXPERIENCE

Working with
Clay, Wire, Wax, Plaster,
and Found Objects

JUDITH PECK, Ed. D.
Associate Professor of Art,
Ramapo College of New Jersey

CHILTON BOOK COMPANY   Radnor, Pennsylvania

Cover: Arlene Beckman (student); dancer in Pariscraft. (Photo by Unhjem/Cavallo.)

Manufactured in the United States of America

Library of Congress Cataloging in Publication Data

Peck, Judith.
      Sculpture as experience: working with clay, wire, wax, plaster,
   and found objects / Judith Peck.
      p.   cm.
      Bibliography: p. 182
      Includes index.
      ISBN 0-8019-7978-1
      1. Sculpture—Technique.   I. Title.
   NB1170.P37   1989
   731.4—dc19   88-43308
                                                       CIP

   5 6 7 8 9 0   8 7 6

This book is dedicated to my mother, who liked the clay cat that I brought home from sixth grade and sent me to spend my Saturday mornings in art school while all the kids on the block were having fun.

Contents

9
Mounting and Finishing

Appendices

Index

Preface

INTEREST in sculpture has grown steadily among Americans in the past two decades. More exhibitions of sculpture appear locally and nationally than ever before, and there is a marked increase in mixed media experimentation in which sculpture is combined with painting and graphic processes. As a result of both the new and ancient technology that is used in the fabrication of contemporary works, sculpture has become increasingly complex. Because of this, it is not unusual to find that individuals who respond well to the direct physical engagement that is usually connected with sculpture-making are somewhat fearful of entering the technical arena in which sculpture seems to function. This book, in its de-emphasis of mechanical methodology, is an invitation to visitors and potential dwellers to enter that arena.

Sculpture as Experience is designed both for students in school who have access to working facilities and for out-of-school adults who will be making space for their creative work at home. The goals of the book are threefold:

1. To introduce students to esthetic concepts of sculptural form and space;
2. To offer instructional guidelines in various three-dimensional media, selected particularly for their potential to help students discover modes of expression suited to their personal artistic direction;
3. To expose students to the special tools, techniques, and methods of sculptural processes that are executed by hand: processes that require a minimum of technology and can be seen through to completion without a fully equipped shop or studio.

Acknowledgments

APPRECIATION is first and foremost extended to my college students, whose enthusiasm and energy for creative expression in sculpture is a continuing source of personal delight and inspiration.

The photographer responsible for most of the illustrations in the text is Lee Vold of Mahwah, New Jersey. I am deeply indebted to Ms. Vold for her high degree of professionalism, perfectionism, efficiency, and sound artistic judgment. Frank Cavallo, Ramapo College Media Technician, provided excellent photographs of several students works, and the Museum of Modern Art was most cooperative in permitting reproduction of works in their collection. All line drawings in the text are by the author.

My colleague, Gordon Bear, is to be thanked for generously guiding me through the mysteries and mastery of word processing. My appreciation for their support is extended to other individuals at Ramapo College: Erik Unhjem, Director of Graphics; Mark Singer, Director of Public Relations: James Hollenbach, Director of the School of Contemporary Arts; Bob Hatala, Vice President for Academic Affairs; and Robert Scott, President.

My thanks go to Lauretta Waligroski, an assistant consistently cooperative and competent, and to Susan Geis and Arvid Knudsen for their individual guidance in the various stages of publication. I am grateful for the support given to my writing by Harvey Peck, and, always, the continuing inspiration of my children Sabrina, Joel, Jennifer, and Sarah.

SCULPTURE
AS
EXPERIENCE

Introduction

You may be somewhat surprised to note the range of methods and materials used to create contemporary sculpture. The sheer number of words employed to describe sculptural activity is impressive. Those that follow will give you some idea of the scope of sculpture and you may discover that you are doing and using many of these things in the course of your own work.

THE SCOPE AND METHODS OF SCULPTURE

Sculpture can be:

- welded in steel;
- carved in wood, stone, cement, and plaster;
- modeled in clay, wax, and plaster;
- fabricated out of found objects;
- constructed out of wood;
- laminated in plastics;
- formed out of rope and fabric;
- beaten out of lead and copper;
- cast in plaster, clay, bronze, stainless steel, aluminum, and plastics;
- pressed in sand;
- dug into the earth;
- conceived and expressed on paper, in words, and in action.

Sculpture can be:

- nailed
- filed
- tied
- wrapped
- painted
- taped
- screwed
- tacked
- hung
- sewn
- balanced
- floated

Fig. I–1. Judith Peck, *Dancing Mother and Child;* bronze, 12″ × 12″ × 9″. (Photo by Lee Vold).

1

- cut
- ground
- sprayed
- glued
- scraped

- drilled
- arranged
- waxed
- sawed
- mounted

Making sculpture is technical in foundation because the process deals with so many physical *things* at every stage, from the preparation of materials and supporting structures, through construction, to final finishing and mounting. Yet, in spite of all its earthbound tribulations, there are few means of creative expression as potentially free in spirit as sculpture. Learning the nature of sculpture's physicality is the key to finding and enjoying that freedom.

Sculpture is experience, for much of what we use to make sculpture we have experienced already and, in fact, are intimately familiar with: the muscles of our body, our senses of touch and sight, our sense of scope in terms of monumentality and detail, and our sense of self in the context of the physical and psychological environment as we confront both the profound and the ordinary. Moreover, the world is three-dimensional and so are we. Sculpture will come as no surprise.

OBJECTIVES OF THE BOOK

This book is presented as experience and not theory. As you work, practical solutions will begin to interest you because sculptural problems will appear as the first handful of clay is pressed between your hands. But problems in art are different than other problems. They are positive in direction. In other words, you are starting from the norm and going upwards, striving for a clearer statement, a greater understanding, a keener awareness. And solving those problems brings you to a higher level of experience.

The primary goal, then, is to provide you with enough information so that you can experience sculpture. A second goal is to provide you with some insight into *seeing*. What you see will directly affect what you make in sculpture. You may think you are seeing when in actuality you are just passing through. For example, you can see the doorway to your home many times a day and never see its physicality. You simply pass through. You can see your face in the mirror many times a day and never see its planes and structure.

Beyond the techniques of sculptural observation that you can learn is the quality of *how* you see, *what* you perceive. And this is not technique. How you see is intimately connected to who you are: what kind of person you are. Are you interested in people, in society, in beauty, in ugliness, in truth? Are you honest in ascertaining what you see and what you feel, and if so, do you have the courage to project that honesty? If not, do you have the constitution to acquire courage? These are not academic questions, nor are they off the track. The person behind the eyes is ultimately the only one who can determine what is finally seen.

THE SCHEDULE: A 15-WEEK PROGRAM

The 15-week sculpture program outlined in this book is based on approximately ten hours of studio work per week. In the classroom, this roughly approximates a school semester. In out-of-school workshop sessions, it is just under a four-month series. If you are working alone, you will, of course, vary your working sessions to meet personal needs: if employed, you may plan on devoting a portion of the weekend and some evenings for studio work; if you have children home, you may have to reduce working time to 20-minute periods, whenever they can be managed (keeping a small work space for kids with a supply of clay is a great idea); you may find that long concentrated sessions work best for you or that short, half-hour sessions stolen from chores are preferable.

Finding the time to work will probably be your first creative challenge, for self-motivated, internally mandated hours do not appear on their own; they must be fabricated. Whether such time is found through the discipline of a regular routine or by salvaging bits and pieces from other sources is largely a matter of individual style.

THE PROJECTS

You will observe, as you move from chapter to chapter, that there are variations in the nature and amount of technical advice given. These variations are due to the differing complexity of the projects and the nature of the objectives in each case. For example, all of the projects are designed to generate personal creative expression through three-dimensional media. Some projects, however, such as *The Figure*

Suggested Schedule in Weeks

Chapter 1. Exercises in Seeing and Drawing
1 week

Chapter 2. Modeling in Clay
1 week

Chapter 3. The Figure in Foil and Pariscraft
1 week

Chapter 4. Found-Object Sculpture   1 week

Chapter 5. Fabricating Wire Sculpture   1 week

Chapter 6. Carving in Plaster, and Cement and Vermiculite   4 weeks

Chapter 7. Making the Head in Clay   4 weeks

Chapter 8. Working in Wax
2 weeks

in Foil and Pariscraft, require that you follow methodical procedures at the outset. Those step-by-step instructions are then followed by more freeform directions. Projects such as *Found-Object Sculpture*, because of the wide-ranging availability of objects, require nonspecific, global advice, equally aesthetic and technical in nature, about choosing and assembling objects for creating sculptures. Still other projects, specifically *Modeling the Head in Clay*, and, to a lesser extent, *Modeling in Clay*, require a more lengthy technical presentation throughout in order to ensure a successful experience. Your personal success in experiencing and completing each project is the objective, and the directives that are offered are toward that end, whether specific or general, lengthy or brief, technical or aesthetic.

It might be reassuring to offer this general advice: although you may find a particular method too difficult or perhaps too easy; a certain medium too expansive or too limited; though you may be satisfied with one product and dissatisfied with another, the experience of actually doing the sculpture remains, with all that that implies—seeing, conceiving, manipulating materials, and producing a concrete object from your imagination. The experience is frustrating often, incomplete sometimes, and ecstatic rarely, but always moving and full of vitality. A state of contentment has never served as inspiration for the making of art.

Photographs of Completed Projects and Art Materials

Almost all of the completed work illustrated was done by students in the author's Basic Sculpture classes, except for sculptures contributed by the Museum of Modern Art and sculptures made by the author. This limitation is deliberate; it is designed to make you aware of the very real possibilities for success in your execution of each project. Many of the students were not art majors, but merely individuals interested in seeing what sculpture was like—something you may be doing as well.

The photographs of tools and materials are intended to illustrate the standard items needed to create each project. To avoid confusing the much-limited space of the photograph, some easily recognizable items mentioned in the *Checklist of Tools and Materials* are not included. Such variables as bases are also not included as they take excessive space and, moreover, will be determined individually in each case.

Extending the Project: Art in Human Service

There is a brief section on "art in human service" at the end of several of the chapters. The material is not offered as a training ground for art therapists; it is much too abbreviated to serve that purpose. Moreover, highly developed skills must accompany the use of art projects in art therapy. Rather, it is offered for those individuals who may be working in a recreational or rehabilitational setting where good creative art activities would benefit the participants. Often, crafts alone or time-consuming busy work is the only fare available, particularly in nursing homes, senior citizen centers, and youth facilities.

The sculpture projects recommended for art in human service, when modified according to the needs and abilities of those participating, are flexible enough to serve disparate groups, do not require an abundance of materials, and incorporate, at once, the hands, mind, senses, and emotions.

Extending the Project: Other Possibilities

Some of the chapters end by suggesting other possible ways to use the projects. You are strongly encouraged to seek out additional possibilities on your own, continually adapting the methods and materials to your evolving artistic ideas.

It is hoped that after trying the various projects, you will discover certain media and methods that you relate to particularly well, and that you will want to continue working in those directions after the 15-week program is completed. An important objective of *Sculpture as Experience* is to expose you to several widely different media, methods, and approaches so that you can make that natural determination. (It is indeed doubtful that you will respond with equal enthusiasm to all of the projects, because of their disparity.)

1 The Dynamics of Sculpture

1 WEEK

ONE WEEK is suggested as the time to devote specifically to exercises in "seeing" with sculptural objectives. However, once you begin doing this, "seeing" with aesthetic judgment should become a natural adjunct to each of the projects described later and serve as an on-going resource for imaginative ideas.

EXERCISES IN SEEING

The exercises given below are designed to increase your visual perception of natural sculptural elements that exist all around you so that you can begin to use those elements dynamically in art-making.

Form, Shape, and Mass

Look around in whatever room you find yourself and select a form, shape, or mass that appeals to you. It might be the light fixture in the ceiling, cracks and scratches on the floor, the curve of the water spigot, or the grid of the radiator. Maybe it will be an open doorway with muted shapes barely seen on the other side, the shadows cast by a fire extinguisher or lamp, the relationship of wall panels to each other or to the floor. It may be the folds caused by the skirt or pants of someone sitting, the vertical variations of a hanging drape, or the heavy outlines of a jacket thrown over a chair. Give expression to each image that you select by simply noting the object and what you like about it. Select at least ten such images. The only criterion for selection is that you respond in a favorable way to the visual impact of the image.

Then look around the room and make note of the forms, shapes and masses that do not appeal to you; ones that you dislike. Try to be as honest as you can in your selections. Seeing is not enough. The forms must be *claimed*. We neither note nor store most of the things we see. But form is

Fig. 1–1. Study the rhythmic flow of lines leading the eye from one figure to another; and the tension created by the lines of the skirt and by the sharp anatomical projections. [Henry Moore, *Family Group* (1948–49); Bronze (cast 1950), 59¼″ × 46½″, 45″ × 29⅞″ at base. Collection, The Museum of Modern Art, New York. A. Conger Goodyear Fund.]

to be your visual vocabulary, so it is time to learn the language.

During the week, do this exercise outdoors if you can; recognize and claim the forms and shapes that give you visual satisfaction. Observe both the natural and the manmade, including trees, skies, landscapes, pavements, buildings, derricks, roadways, and so on.

Tension, Contrast, and Design

Place your hands in front of you. Make a fist and see how the bone presses against the soft skin, forming tension at the knuckles and lyrical curves between the knuckles. Make shapes using your hands and fingers: claw shapes, extended fingers, bent fingers. See how the tension between forms creates a contrast between straight and curved, flat and rounded.

Now, move both hands together in relation to one another. Imagine that they are large sculptural forms mounted in interrelationship. There are solid areas and there are hollow areas. Play the symmetry of the fingers against the solid masses of the palm and wrist. Contrast highs and lows. Have one hand work as an inner form within the other. Enclose space by closing some of the lines of the fingers and creating a form within a form. Each time you change these relationships try to observe, as much as possible, all that is going on in terms of design, and note the relationships that particularly appeal to you.

Observe people sitting and standing in a room. Notice how knees press against skirts and pant legs, forcing the drape of the material to cascade into folds. There are a myriad of high points and strong points (tension points) in the drape and pull of clothing against the body. Dancers use the extra dimension of costuming as an extension of the body's capability for creating tension, contrast, and design in space.

Line, Balance, and Rhythm

Stand in front of others in a room or stand alone in front of a full-length mirror. Notice how you present a vertical image and are in symmetry with most of the things around you: seated or standing people, tables, chairs, pictures on the wall. Everything is in order. Now, suddenly thrust yourself in a diagonal as if you were about to fall. If you are in front of the room notice how everyone perks up and takes interest. This is not because they wanted to see you fall on your face but because you were off balance, and that is an exciting dynamic. You created a diagonal line with your body—an action line. We are bilaterally symmetric when we come into the world, and that is our viewpoint in all that we observe. When a picture is crooked on the wall, we can't wait to right it. When figures are off balance, they are off the norm and visually exciting. Lines can be used in sculpture in dramatic ways—not lines that are incised into forms but the exterior and interior lines made by the interaction of forms; lines, in effect, that will form the integral designs of your sculpture.

Essentially, rhythm in art has to do with the movement of line in a given space; the contrasting design, for example, of straight lines and curves, highs and lows, ins and outs. The rhythms you design can lead the viewer's eye in a visual tempo of your own making, as lyrical as a Debussy piano movement or as strong and intense as a Wagnerian opera. Just as you feel rhythm in music and dance, often to the point of moving your body to its engaging patterns, so will you feel rhythm in the emerging sculptural forms of your imagination. Nature is the best advisor on this subject: refer especially to the visual rhythms in trees, rivers, birds, animals, and people as they walk, turn, engage in sports, and dance (figure 1–2). Be alert to the special rhythms that perform for you in daily life, ordinary movements such as the shifts and turns of a deft short order cook behind a busy counter during lunch hour.

During the week make a list of at least ten such designs in the natural or human environment—designs that appeal to you. Then, with pencil and paper, see if you can isolate the essential rhythmic lines in five of your selections: that is, the curves, straight lines, and other contrasts as indicated above. Alter the lines if you can make them more exciting by emphasizing the contrasts.

Looking around the room again, review the forms you originally selected as ones you liked. With pencil and paper try to find the rhythmic lines within those forms. Simplify the lines as much as possible. Repeat the exercise with other objects or relationships that appeal to you. During the week find reproductions from library books on sculpture and modern dance that have especially lyrical or otherwise dynamic designs. Draw, in simple lines, the basic rhythms that form each composition.

This is not a test. The lines you see may be different

Fig. 1–2. Observe the designs in space made by the human body. Alice Teirstein, dancer. (Photo by Mariette Pathy Allen.)

from those seen by someone else. None of the exercises have right or wrong answers. Their purpose is to engage you in a feeling for rhythm and balance in sculpture and help you incorporate those elements naturally into your work. You might begin by searching for some of the rhythmic lines in *Family Group* by Henry Moore (figure 1–1), and *Man in the Open Air* by Eli Nadelman (figure 1–3).

Texture, Light, and Shadow

Texture adds other dimensions to the quality of a sculpture and extends its visual impact. The highly polished steel surface of Jose de Rivera's *Construction 8* (figure 1–4) reflects

Fig. 1–3. Study the lines in this composition for rhythm and balance. Note the stylized contours that create a lyrical design, and the impact of light and shadow. [Elie Nadelman, *Man in the Open Air* (c. 1915); Bronze, 54½″ high, 11¾″ × 21½″ at base. Collection, The Museum of Modern Art, New York. Gift of William S. Paley.]

Fig. 1–4. The lines of this sculpture are flowing and unending, with light reflections continually changing as the sculpture revolves on its base. [José de Rivera, *Construction 8.* (1954); Stainless steel forged rod, 9⅜" high. Collection, The Museum of Modern Art, New York. Gift of Mrs. Heinz Schultz in memory of her husband.]

the surrounding colors and shadows. Texture aids the fluidity of movement in Eli Nadelman's suave *Man in the Open Air*, where the light is forced to play upon the sculpture according to the artist's baton. Textures extend the personality of the stylish *Schrafftsperson* by the author (figure 1–5), her flamboyant hat, scarf, and sandals emphasized by contrasting polished highlights.

Texture can provide new sources of interest within a sculpture. In figure 1–6, for example, roughly textured patterns contrast with a smoothly sanded surface.

Texture, light, and shadow, though they may add dimension to the sculpture, must evolve from the sculpture. They must be in concert with the other vital elements of the work. As an exercise, find those textures and shadows in the room that appeal to you and those that do not. Is there an object in the room (or beyond the room, through the window) that does not seem to you to have integrity of texture, that appears inconsistent with other formal elements? In your research during the week, seek out examples of textures that add dimension, emphasis, meaning, or dramatic impact to a work of sculpture. Do the same with regard to the dramatic impact produced by light and shadow.

Fig. 1–5. Contrasting textures add interest and extend the personality of the figure through the costuming. Swirled patterns in the body of the sculpture contrast with smooth, highly polished accessories that catch the light. [Judith Peck, *Schrafftsperson* (1976); Bronze. 16″ high, 7″ × 7″ at base. Collection, Mr. and Mrs. Henry Solan. (Photo by Jules Pinsley).]

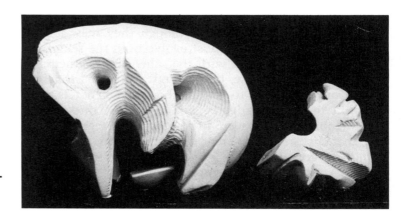

Fig. 1–6. Texture is an integral part of this design: deeply carved "stripes" form the hollows while smooth flat areas demarcate the surface planes. [Gary Smith (student), *Space Shuttle*; Plaster. (Photo by Lee Vold)]

Spatial Relationships

Ask five people to line up in a room. Divide the people in a number of different ways, observing *all* the changes made in the *space surrounding the figures* as they move to different positions. Here are some suggestions:

1. Place people in a line with an even distribution of space between them.
2. Place people in a line, separating the two end figures and bunching three together in the middle.
3. Place people in a line, bunching the end figures together on either side and isolating the middle figure within the empty space.
4. Place three people in a circle on their knees and two outside the circle, standing.
5. Place four people in a line, one behind the other and one randomly placed, apart.
6. Move the line-up above to one side of the room and place the random figure alone in the center space.

It is interesting to note that the space changes its visual dimensions as the figures change their relationship to one another. It can become more square, more rectangular, smaller, larger, denser, narrower, wider. The space can become more interesting and less interesting as well.

Now, if you have a willing group, take turns in changing the relationships of the figures and surrounding space by moving the figures from the vertical to other angles, such as diagonal and horizontal. Use bent torso and extended limbs. Try to note the design ingredients of contrast, tension, line, rhythm, and balance in space. If you are one of the figures, try to feel these designs in your body as they are being projected.

In your research, examine (either in person or through photographs) sculptural group compositions (figurative or abstract) and single abstract monumental sculptures that have been installed in public places. Try to relate what you have physically participated in to what you see. Observe where compositions are lifeless and where they have force and vitality. Examine again figure 1–1, Henry Moore's *Family Group*, and try to isolate the design ingredients described above.

EXERCISES IN DRAWING

The exercises offered below are an expansion of the experiences in visual perception that you have just had. In these exercises, do not think of drawing as a technique to be learned, but rather as a way of implementing the natural elements of sculpture in an easy way, without having to lift heavy objects with a crane, weld with a torch, or carve with a pneumatic chisel. Approach the studies as if you were creating a large sculpture, organizing form, shape, and line, but without the massive effort that making a heroic sculpture would entail.

Two Relating Forms

Using a narrow and a medium-wide brush dipped in black ink or watercolor and a large sheet of paper, paint several examples of *two forms in interrelationship*. Use sweeping movements to make definitive lines and shapes. The lines and shapes need not be complex, and you need not spend a great amount of time perfecting them. Use one or more of the ingredients of contrast, tension, rhythm, balance, opposing lines, and any of the other elements of sculptural design that you have been observing. Be alert to both the positive and negative forms that are created: positive forms are the filled-in masses; negative forms are created by the empty spaces or voids between the masses.

Lines can be closed to form shapes; shapes can be filled to form masses. Make at least six spatial studies and spread them out on the floor so that they can be seen from all angles. Thinking about what has been produced in terms of the formal design components of the drawings will increase your perception of the relationship of forms in space.

By making these studies and analyzing them, you are confronting many of the same visual problems the sculptor confronts but without the technical problems of making the piece stand, connect, work from all sides, and have permanence. This exercise can save a great deal of time by increasing your understanding of what is strong and exciting in sculpture and what is weak and without impact. Illustrated in figure 1–7 is Henry Moore's *Ideas for Two-Figure Sculpture*, which is as much a study of the relationship of forms as it is figures. In your drawings, think *only* of forms. If representational ideas are summoned from the forms that you produce, only then carry them forward.

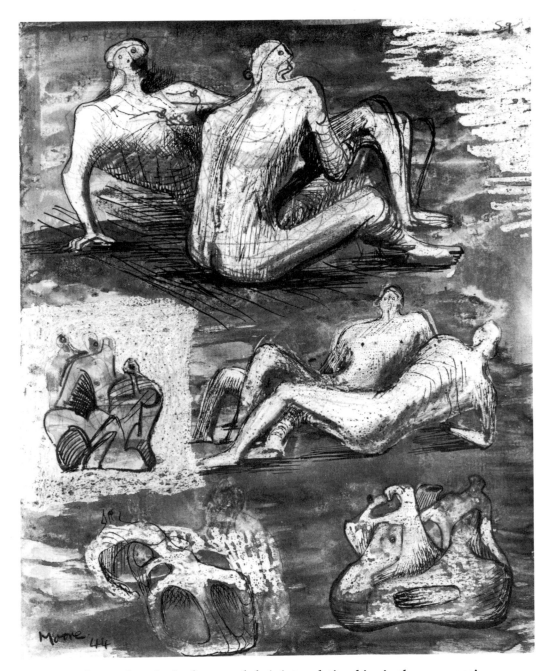

Fig. 1–7. Isolate and study the forms and their interrelationships in these compositions. [Henry Moore, *Ideas for Two-Figure Sculpture* (1944); Crayon, pen and ink, pencil, watercolor, $8\frac{7}{8}'' \times 6\frac{7}{8}''$. Collection, The Museum of Modern Art, New York. Purchase.]

Fig. 1–8. An example of a freeform "scribble" from which ideas for sculpture were generated. [Unidentified student drawing with felt tip marker. (Photo by Lee Vold).]

Freeform Scribble

With a pencil or conte crayon on any sheet of paper 12″ × 18″ or larger, make a free-wheeling scribble. Do not look for anything at the outset, just scribble. When you have enough lines on the paper, look at your markings carefully and then begin to select certain lines to bring out. Forms can be developed by combining lines, and masses can be made by shading in areas. The scribble lines can be used as a takeoff point, or added to, or selected out and darkened. Whether you develop lines, forms, masses, or all three will depend on what you see in the markings and what you want to emphasize. Figure 1–8 is an example of this exercise.

PERSONAL VISION

The conclusion you may reach after a week of "seeing" and drawing in the ways suggested may be that you *do* have a distinctive way of seeing. You respond consistently to certain forms, rhythms, and patterns.

If your responses are successful enough to form the basis of good artistic judgment, you are off to a good start. If, however, the extent of your involvement with forms and shapes has been restricted to functional objects, you may find your aesthetic judgment lacking. For example, you may only be at home with symmetry and familiar geometric shapes because you lack visual association with forms and designs other than commercial household goods and furnishings. Once you begin consciously looking for and reacting to form, design, and other sculptural stimuli, you will start to develop a good vocabulary of visual awareness. As you continue to work, in whatever sculptural medium you come to prefer, you will find this vocabulary indispensable in helping you establish what you want to say and how you intend to say it.

Style

In this chapter, we have tried to isolate the formal components of sculpture so that the elements may be understood. Once it is clear that sculpture involves these components (form, shape, mass, line, tension, contrast, design, rhythm, balance, texture, space, light, and shadow) you will be ready to try both abstract and representational styles.

Style in art is using the formal components in a given medium to communicate a personal statement. Style, as well as content, communicates the artist's "message," if indeed there is one. A consistent personal style in a body of work evolves only after working for a substantial period of time in a medium and understanding its possibilities. Some of the considerations that may form the basis for achieving a personal style in sculpture are offered here, not as specific guidelines but as a general overview:

Learning what can be done with given materials.
Exploring space with an eye for sculptural composition.
Comprehending the concepts of dynamic design and an integrated composition.
Thinking in sculptural imagery.
Becoming familiar with the scope of contemporary sculptural expression in gallery and museum exhibitions, outdoor installations, and public buildings.

Abstract or Representational

It is easier to begin the practical study of studio sculpture by proceeding with abstract rather than representational images. Working to get something to look like something else tends to undermine your ability to experiment with all the considerations of form that were described in this chapter. When the formal components are understood and integrated into your artistic activity, you should, and hopefully will, express whatever you wish in whatever way you wish. The dynamics of sculpture are just as forceful and convincing in a good abstract piece as they are in a good representational piece.

It is important not to block off any one area of sculpture as being unworthy of your interest. Innovative media, including telecommunications, performance pieces, conceptual pieces, earthworks, and so on, all serve to enrich the environment of sculptural possibility. You need not select any of them as your way. Anger, impatience, frustration, and disgust are honest emotions and are sometimes entirely appropriate. Only intolerance is to be avoided because it will distance you too much to draw anything from your experience.

Content

Content has not been discussed in this chapter nor will it be, as there are virtually no limitations on the content of sculpture. The vocabulary here is as rich as the individual's awareness of self, society, culture, and history. It cannot be learned in an art class or an art book, although any learning adds to its store.

Art is a synthesis of idea, visual vocabulary, style, meaning, communication, and the artist's projection of his or her physical, emotional, and intellectual energy. The process and the end results are inexorably connected. Sculpture—its materials, tools, techniques, language, and structure—must be experienced and practiced. One should approach the practical study of studio sculpture as an adventurous process and as a means to an artistic end, with results that may be of significance to oneself and to others.

Modeling in Clay 2

1 WEEK

THE limited time allocated should encourage spontaneity in working with this versatile medium, yet be sufficient to begin to make you familiar with the medium. In this time period you might do a single piece or two or three sketches, depending on your personal inclination and mode of attack.

THE NATURE OF THE PROJECT

Clay is a flexible medium. This can be good or bad for beginners: good because clay responds to every push, pull, and pat; bad because it offers so little resistance that all direction must come from outside forces, namely you. Little guidance derives from the medium as, for example, in carving or in welding, where the rigidity of the material forms a basis for attack. The sculptor's approach in manipulating structurally solid media such as stone, wood, and steel is predicated to some extent on existing forms: removing masses in carving; organizing shapes in welding. With clay there are no existing structures other than those you create. This means that you must develop a good sense of the formal dynamics of sculpture to deter you from going in too many confusing directions at once.

Nevertheless, with clay, as with all sculptural media, a healthy respect for the material is necessary. Yes, it follows your direction, but only to the point of its own limitations, and those limitations are critical. Understanding the techniques of clay modeling, as with most sculptural techniques, is initially a matter of plunging in and working.

This chapter on modeling in clay refers to clay work for kiln firing; therefore, water-base clay is the medium described. Water-base clay, even when dry and hard, is not permanent; it crumbles easily and will revert to its mud state when wet. Oil-base clay or plastiline (which cannot be fired) never dries; it remains flexible. Sculpture made in both water-base and oil-base clay can be made permanent and, in

Fig. 2–1. In modeling, observe that round forms as
well as flat shapes are more
evenly made with the
wooden block and wooden
blade of the tool than with
the fingers. [Paul Barbier,
Duck; Fired clay. (Photo by
Lee Vold).]

addition, duplicates can be made by the process of casting:
preparing a plaster mold of the sculpture and making a cast
of it in liquid materials that become hard when set such as
plaster, hydrocal, clay slip, concrete, and thermosetting resins. Preparing such casts can be done in the home studio
(see *References* for book resources on casting.) Casting in
metal is done in foundries specially designed for sculpture
casting. (See *References* for bronze foundries.)

In clay modeling, as in other projects described in sub-
sequent chapters, try not to become too frustrated or put off
by the myriad of "looking fors" that constantly appear to
engage your energies while you are working: looking for the
proper size wood to prop a sagging form; looking for a larger
base on which to work; looking for a decent plastic for wrapping. In sculpture, one works with things—a lot of things—
and these, in turn, are supported by other things. Clay modeling involves only a moderate amount of things to be concerned with in comparison with other sculpture techniques,
but one must expect and allow for time to be spent in setting
up and cleaning up materials and in the interminable "look-

ing fors" in between. Advance planning and good organization will help, of course, but in the throes of creative work those qualities do not regularly appear. Even experienced sculptors get bogged down, searching, gathering, adding supports. Therefore, patience and fortitude are the virtues to be sought. Because sculpture is physical, it uses a lot of energy, and that energy is not always required nor spent in the forward push.

THE BASIC MEDIUM

Several firing clays are suitable for sculpture. Two generally available clays are Jordon Buff with grog (a light tan) and Terra Cotta with grog (a deep red). Clay is most economically purchased in fifty-pound cartons, each consisting of two twenty-five-pound plastic-wrapped bags.

Oven-firing clay is clay that does not require firing in a kiln but instead is baked in an ordinary home oven. It is more expensive and smoother in consistency than those recommended above. Avoid "non-firing clay," sold in hobby shops, as it is rubbery and difficult to work artistically.

Grog is prefired clay that is ground into small particles and mixed evenly through the firing clay. It reduces the risk of breakage in the kiln by creating pores through which moisture can escape; it also helps to modify shrinkage as, having already been fired, the grog can no longer shrink. Grog serves another purpose: it creates a mildly granular texture that inhibits the slick finish that beginners sometimes attempt at the expense of form when they first approach the medium. The amount of grog in commercially premixed clay is normally from 20 to 30 percent, and the particle size is usually medium grain. Both the proportion and the particle size can be custom ordered, or clay and grog can be bought separately and mixed to fit special requirements.

The clay and modeling tools can be found in sculpture supply houses (see *Sources of Supply*). The remaining tools and materials are available in household goods or hardware stores.

CHECKLIST OF TOOLS AND MATERIALS

The equipment discussed here is shown in figures 2–2 and 2–3:

- Small wooden blocks: cut from scraps in assorted sizes, $\frac{1}{4}$ inch to 1 inch thick; used as initial hand tools in forming the sculpture. The blocks also serve as props for support while working.
- Wooden paddle: useful for packing clay and solidifying the forms. A thin, flat piece of wood is an acceptable substitute.
- Wooden modeling tools: tools with thin, flat surfaces and slightly curved rounded ends are particularly useful. Modeling tools begin where the small blocks leave off: to press, shape, carve, curve, and direct the forms.
- Wire-ended tools: most practical are tools with wire inserted on one end and the flat wooden surface described above on the other. The wire is a carving implement, triangular, with one surface serrated, the other flat (figure 2–3), used to define shapes and contours and to control surface textures.
- Plastic modeling tools: these are sold as a set and are useful for detail because of their thin blades and flexibility.
- Turntable or lazy Susan: used to turn work in progress so that it can be easily seen from all sides (not shown).
- Rags, plastic bag, and plastic wrap (heavy duty): for keeping clay damp while work is in progress (not shown).

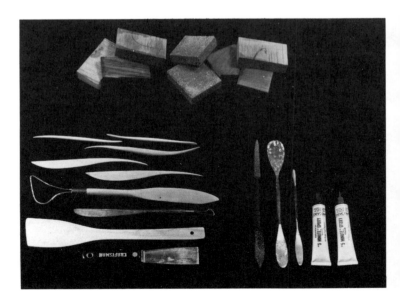

Fig. 2–2. Tools and materials for clay modeling. (Photo by Erik Unhjem and Frank Cavallo).

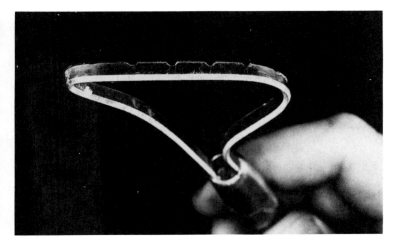

Fig. 2–3. A wire-ended tool, one edge serrated and the other flat, is used to carve the clay and help you define the shapes and contours of your work. (Photo by Unhjem/Cavallo).

- Plaster bat: for drying out clay if excessively moist (optional, not shown).
- Spatula: for dispensing clay and for cleanup.
- Metal file: for repairs after firing, as needed.
- Five-Minute Epoxy: for repairs after firing, as needed.
- Plastic bins (2): for storing clay. One is used to reconstitute dry clay; the other is used to store clay that is ready for modeling. Covered plastic garbage bins are adequate (not shown).

PREPARATION OF CLAY AND WORKSPACE

Clean the surface on which you will be working, as loose particles of debris may mix with the clay and cause damage during kiln firing. Any flat surface will do. You may sit or stand, as you prefer, but your work should be at a height convenient for your hands to work without strain and should be positioned so that you are not looking down upon it but directly at it. This is important as sculptural forms cannot be seen clearly unless there is open space around them.

Obtaining the Right Consistency

The moist clay should be of good working consistency without the need to add or evaporate moisture. Sometimes clay is too moist or too dry to work easily. If only moderately "sticky," proceed to wedge the clay and get to work, as most excess moisture will air dry within the first hour of working. If, however, the clay sticks to the working surface and will not wedge, it may be flattened out on plaster bats or a reasonably clean cement floor from which loose particles of plaster, paint, or other debris have been swept away. The excess moisture will be absorbed from under the clay as the air dries it from above; flipping it over will hasten drying. The clay is ready for working when it does not stick excessively to your hands or the work surface, but is nevertheless soft and malleable. Use a wide, flat spatula to lift the clay; avoid chipping the plaster bats, as plaster mixed with clay is dangerous in kiln firing.

If the clay is too dry, wrap it in a damp rag and cover it securely with a plastic bag. The clay must remain wrapped overnight to be easily handled for modeling (assuming that it is only a little dry and not hard and lumpy, in which case the clay must be reconstituted (see below under "Repairs").

Wedging the Clay

Wedging is a process of compressing clay particles to remove air bubbles. Pockets of air remaining when the sculpture is finished and dry can cause the piece to explode in the kiln. Hollowing (described later) substantially reduces this risk; wedging at the outset is a double precaution.

1. Cut off a substantial amount of clay from the block with a piece of wire.
2. Clean the working surface and position yourself higher than the clay mound for body leverage.
3. Throw the clay into a ball or rectangle by slamming it down on your counter surface. This should be done repeatedly and is usually an adequate method of wedging for sculpture.

Another way of wedging, used by potters and suited to delicate modeling projects where later hollowing is not intended is this:

1. Take an amount of clay that fits comfortably in your hands and form a ball.
2. Press the ball down and away from you in a rocking motion so that the clay nearest to you tilts up behind the heel of your hand.
3. Rock the ball back toward you and pivot it slightly; then, without lifting it, press again in a rocking motion, squeezing down with the heel of your hand and

again tilting up the clay nearest you. The clay "flap" that appears behind the heel of your hand works itself into the ball each time you pivot and press. In this manner, the clay is compressed and air bubbles are squeezed out.

4. Repeat the motion until you have made two full circles in your pivots.

Whichever method of wedging you use, prepare at least two mounds, one for your initial shape and another one for adding to it.

PROCEDURES FOR WORKING IN CLAY

As you work, the following procedures and precautions are necessary. They are fine points but technically essential, so it is a good idea to refer to them periodically as you move from conception to completion to cleanup and prepare to begin again:

- Keep a damp rag around the extra mound of clay so that it does not dry and get hard.
- Collect all small scraps of clay and press them together. Keep this mound under the damp rag as well.
- Particles of dry clay in your sculpture can cause air bubbles and breakage in firing; therefore, do not add them to your mound but put them back in the clay bin (a closed container, covered with a wet rag, used to remoisten clay).
- Dry clay should be scraped from tools before they are used, for the reason stated above and because a tool is no longer a tool when it is covered with clay. Therefore, scrape wet clay frequently from tools and put that clay under the damp rag also.
- When you are leaving the sculpture for any length of time it is wise to cover it, unless it is very wet and you want it to dry out. If you are leaving the piece for several days, wrap it in a damp rag and cover that with a plastic covering. Bind the plastic at the bottom with a wire or wrap the plastic under your working base so that the sculpture remains air tight.
- If the piece is left for longer than a week, it should be checked and rewrapped if necessary. Do not work on a dry piece, as the fresh clay will peel off or crack. Su-

perficial wetting is of no value when the piece is dry, as the outer layer of moisture will quickly evaporate.

- Thoroughly dry clay intended for reuse must be reconstituted (a process described later).
- Clay can clog the sink drain. It is therefore wise to first wash clay-covered hands and tools in a pail of water. Then let clay water sit until the clay rests on the bottom before pouring off the water. The residual clay is reusable.

FORMING THE SCULPTURE

As you manipulate the clay, experiment with the various tools at your disposal and carefully observe the unlimited variety of possible effects. Forming the sculpture involves a great deal of *looking*. More than half your time, in fact, may be spent looking and not working.

Looking I: The Initial Shape

Achieving an interesting beginning shape is a significant first step. Throw one of the mounds of clay onto your surface. Throw it several times until a shape that interests you appears. (This process might already have occurred in the wedging.) The shape may be rectangular, triangular, amoeboid, square, oval, or circular. Whatever shape you arrive at, it is a good idea to elongate the initial form to allow for some settling or "squatting" of the soft clay as it is worked. Now press the mound onto your lazy Susan so that it will be easy to view from all sides as you proceed.

An alternative way to form the initial shape is to prepare two clay mounds and combine them. The two forms may make an intriguing structure to start off with. When combining the two forms, roughen the surfaces first and press them together well. (At this point the mounds are soft and will not need slip—a mixture described later—to join them.)

Using the Small Wooden Block

The wooden block should fit comfortably in your hand; it need not be a specific shape or thickness. Use the edges as well as the surface of the block and make planes as you work the clay. Take note of the shapes and masses that appeal to you as they form. You may not use all or any of the shapes that emerge as you play with the wooden block against the clay mound, but they become part of your visual vocabulary for future use. Cut into the clay with the edges of the block, continuing to make a mental note of the forms that interest you.

Now begin to relate the important masses. Do not be concerned with details at this point. If the block is soft and sagging, push in an upward direction as you work with the wood. If it is too soft, set it aside without wrapping and begin to work on another clay mound. Begin as before by slamming that into an interesting shape and paddling to solidify the forms.

Adding Clay

In adding clay as you work, it is helpful to roll a pellet of clay between your hands before pressing it on. This slight movement makes the clay more compact and of better consistency. It also gives you a chance to look at the sculpture for another moment before pressing on more clay. When you have built up a form, pat the additional clay with your paddle or wood. A structural solidness, whatever the shape, is what you are striving for.

Looking II: Step Back

It is impossible to see your work only at close range. As indicated earlier, sculpture must have space around it for the forms to be seen.

Periodically, it is wise to step far back from the sculpture (across the room if possible) so that all details disappear and only the large forms are in viewing range. Decisions are constantly being made in sculpture, and they cannot be made without seeing and recognizing the problems.

Looking III: Turn the Sculpture Frequently

Do not finish first one side and then another. Anything done on one side of your sculpture will surely affect the other, and changes will occur continually as you work because of those changing relationships. Remember also that there are not merely four sides to a sculpture; all views count within a 360-degree radius. Include the bird's eye and worm's eye views in your looking, as every view will affect the ultimate form. To turn the piece comfortably, secure the base of the lazy Susan to the working surface with a few daubs of clay so that only the upper disc moves.

Using Wooden Tools to Shape Forms and Create Planes

A good tool is said to be an extension of the hand, and this is certainly true in clay modeling. Hands can compress the clay and fingers can apply clay and shape the masses, but hands and fingers cannot do the job completely because they are rounded and soft. Wooden tools, properly shaped, can form planes, which solidify and crystallize the forms so that the sculpture is not just a mass of undistinguished blobs. A well-structured round form is just as easily made with a wooden blade as is a flat shape, and it will, in fact, be more evenly rounded than if it were formed with your fingers and hands (see figure 2–1).

Where planes meet, high points or depressions are formed with distinct sculptural characteristics, such as ridges, curves, hollows, and other shapes. These intersections cast shadows, which form much of the impact and vitality of sculpture (figure 2–4). Try to train yourself to see forms in terms of planes and the way planes meet, rather than as unfathomable mounds, bumps, and grooves.

To make planes, press the wooden tool against the clay and apply the pressure you need to shape the forms. Use the cutting edges of the tools to carve away and model the areas where planes meet.

Fig. 2–4. Note the high points and boldly carved depressions, which create dramatic cast shadows in this abstract figure sculpture. [Paul Landy (student), Untitled; Fired clay. (Photo by Unhjem/Cavallo).]

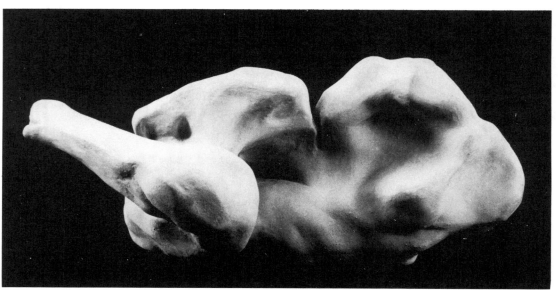

Shaping the Large Masses

Attention must be given to the outer contours of the clay mound. You will be building out at times and carving in at other times to create movement, contrast, and balance. Negative spaces (openings) can be cut into the mound and can also be developed into shapes (figure 2–5). The internal form of those shapes is defined by the surrounding structures.

Look carefully at the forms that are emerging. Could a form extend farther or move deeper or be more angular or become more rounded? Develop a single form fully, carrying it around to other sides. Consider making variations on some forms to place in other parts of the sculpture. Develop variations for both positive and negative spaces.

Fig. 2–5. The contours of this abstraction are formed by the internal or negative spaces as well as the external shape. [Jonathan Richter (student), Untitled; Unfired clay. (Photo by Lee Vold).]

Style

Try for stylistic consistency. For example, an anatomically realistic limb modeled on an abstract figure will probably result in a stylistically inconsistent piece. Forms can have contrast (such as flat against curved, sharp against round, rough against smooth) and still have stylistic consistency, whereas detailed, delicate designs together with bold, roughly-hewn or jagged shapes might be inconsistent in style.

If a realistic image is expressed, does it still project strong and interesting forms in space, apart from its subject matter? Would another person be likely to say, "That is a good cat" rather than "That is a good sculpture?" Figures 2–1, 2–6 and 2–7 are illustrations of stylistically consistent sculptures.

Working with the Accident

As you work, some shapes that emerge will be rejected by you immediately and others will be carried forward to be

Fig. 2–6. The bird is elaborately decorated in repetitive patterns but without sacrifice to form or design. [Karin Baumohl (student), *Bird*; Unfired clay. (Photo by Lee Vold).]

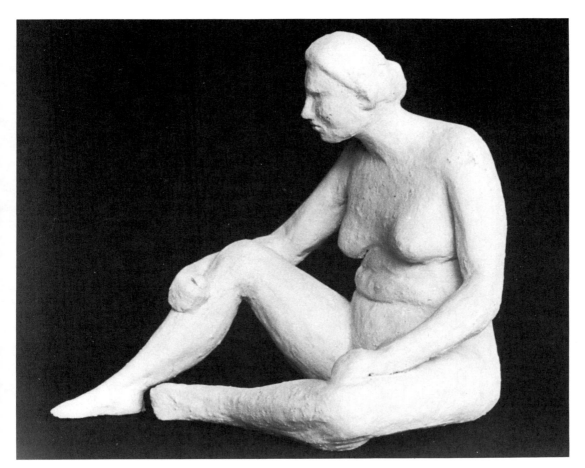

extended, exaggerated, distorted, and so on. You are quite naturally experimenting with form in a trial-and-error way, since only as forms emerge can they be seen and assessed and related to the piece as a whole. Being new to sculpture, you are not bringing images *to* your work so much as finding them *as* you work. But sooner or later, you will begin to crystallize your forms, define directions, and feel that you know what you are doing.

Then, something may happen that you did not intend. Perhaps you cut too far or something may fall off, or someone's elbow may smash into the front. Before you surrender to the mishap, look carefully, for accidents can be significant events in the creative process. Lacking courage, we sometimes subconsciously even cause accidents to happen so that

Fig. 2–7. The planes are simplified and well structured in this seated figure. [Unidentified student sculpture. (Photo by Lee Vold).]

we will be forced to act strongly. Try using the accident as a new possibility, a new direction. Remember that often, in our timidity, we rely on those physical images with which we are familiar and comfortable in creating sculptural forms. An accident, no matter how strange it may first appear to the eye, can cause you to leave some of those tired images and see things with a fresh and spontaneous eye. The next step is to begin to have confidence in the new images that are forming in your head and try them out as well.

Your art is rarely "ruined." Yes, when it blows up in the kiln, the work is ruined (though even then, remarkable things have been known to emerge from the shards). But as long as *you* are not ruined, the process goes on. The process in art is valid at every step along the way. Even though you may ultimately reject the product, the process of making it was an experience that remains. The sculpture was worked and formal aesthetic decisions were made, some of which may appear in other combinations in future work.

REPAIRS

This section covers reconstituting dry clay to a moist and malleable condition and repairing sculptures both while you are working on them and after firing.

Reconstituting Dry Clay

A separate, covered plastic container should be used for reconstituting clay when it is too dry to use. With a hammer, break the clay into small pieces; cover the clay with water, then close the container. When the clay has absorbed the water (a large amount takes several days), bail out the excess water. Form the sticky clay into mounds. Use plaster bats to help absorb the excess moisture; then knead the clay until it is the right consistency for modeling. A second airtight bin should be used for storage of ready-to-use clay.

Using Slip

Slip is a mixture of clay and water, mixed to the consistency of heavy cream. It can be made and stored in a covered container or simply mixed on the spot.

You will use slip to attach parts that crack or fall off the form. You will also use it to add parts to the form, unless the clay is so soft that additions adhere easily. You can use slip if your sculpture becomes "dumpy" and you want to elongate it by adding a mound of clay to a desired thickness at the base. Never glue parts together if you expect to fire the piece, as glue does not behave like clay in the kiln.

How to use slip:

1. Prepare the edges to be joined by crosshatching both sides with your wooden tool.
2. Add a coating of slip and wriggle the two sides together so that slip oozes out of the crevice.
3. Pinch the sides all around the joint, pulling the top of the joint to the bottom and the bottom to the top.
4. Fill the depression between the joint with more clay, bringing it flush with the rest of the piece.
5. If the extremity added or repaired was slender, it is wise to cover that area with plastic while continuing to work. If the mended area dries too quickly it might break off again.

Breakage after Firing

If small parts break off in firing they can be repaired. Parts can also be repaired if they break off when the kiln load is ready and there is no time to go through the wetting and drying process of slip application. In each case, the piece is fired together with its parts and put back together later in the following manner:

1. With a metal file, scrape some particles of fired clay from the bottom of your sculpture onto the table surface.
2. Mix a small amount of quick setting epoxy resin and hardener per package directions. Use a nail or a wooden coffee stirrer to avoid skin contact and apply the resin to the joint; then wriggle the parts together so that the resin oozes to the edge of the seam. Again using an implement or a plastic glove, apply the particles you have scraped so that the seam is covered. Be careful not to disturb the setting process as you do this.

DRYING: HOLLOWING AND STORAGE

Slow and even drying is the key to safe drying, drying without cracks. In order for the sculpture to be allowed to shrink in the drying process, it must be hollowed out while it is still damp. As a general guideline, a thickness of approximately one inch throughout is desirable. Thicknesses less than that do not require hollowing.

Hollowing

Hollowing is accomplished as follows:

1. Wait until the piece has lost most of its softness so that it will not cave in.
2. Hold the piece (if it is small) or lay it down on its least elaborate side, on a surface with some give (rags will do).
3. With your large wire and wooden tool, scoop out the clay from the bottom. Use both ends of the tool: the wire for digging out the middle and reaching up into the form and the wood for scraping out a neat inner wall.
4. Try not to puncture the outer wall. View the exterior form as a directional guide, inserting your tool inside and then out to see how deeply you have gone (figure 2–8). Strive for a 1-inch thick wall.
5. If a form is difficult to hollow and not especially thick, insert a long thin stick into it and out again so that some air space will be made to accommodate shrinkage. A pin hole at the top of the form, to allow steam to escape, is also a good idea.

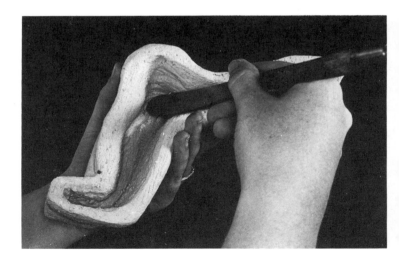

Fig. 2–8. While hollowing, insert your tool inside and then outside of the form to judge how deeply you have gone. (Photo by Unhjem/Cavallo).

6. When the form is thick and needs hollowing but is inaccessible from underneath, has no designated bottom, or is too large to manipulate, it must be hollowed in another way: remove a slice of the form near the inaccessible area, hollow the form, and replace the slice with slip in the manner described for repairs. (Figures 7–16 to 7–20 illustrate this procedure, which is followed after modeling a head in clay.)

Storage

Place the sculpture on two evenly thick slats of wood so that air can circulate under as well as around it. The wood slats need be no more than ¾ inch thick but should be placed far enough apart so that there is a flow of air.

Begin air drying the sculpture by placing a loose plastic covering over it, so that the top will not dry more quickly than the bottom. (The plastic can be removed when the piece begins drying throughout.) The sculpture must be bone dry inside and out before firing (you will know it is dry when the color changes) but do not dry it quickly or unevenly by placing it near a radiator or in the hot sun. Even when the sculpture appears completely dry it will still need slow kiln drying at a low setting to remove all moisture.

PLANNING FOR KILN FIRING AND ALTERNATIVES

As stated earlier, clay, even in its hardened state, is not permanent. It will crack and crumble and if moistened sufficiently, will revert to its original mud condition. Firing the clay (baking it in a very hot oven) causes chemical changes in the clay body that make it permanent. Indeed, fired clay sculptures and pottery have endured for centuries.

Nevertheless, firing your sculpture may present problems because kilns are not always readily available for your use. The following section addresses that problem.

Kiln Firing

It is doubtful that you will invest in a kiln in the early stages of your experience with clay. If you do, it will be purchased according to your individual needs and available space. Therefore, information on firing technique is not given here. Procedures for firing will, in any case, vary according to the type of clay used, the size of the kiln, and the amount, size and type of work being fired. Should you decide to purchase a kiln, the dealer can provide adequate information (see *Sources of Supply* for kilns and kiln furniture).

Adaptive Clay Selection

You may have access to a high school or college kiln, or local ceramic facilities might be willing to fire your work for a fee. Different clays fire at different temperatures; it is wise, therefore, to try to make arrangements for firing at the outset so that you can plan to use the same clay that the school or the ceramic facility uses. Then wedge, construct, and hollow your first piece with care so that your craftsmanship will be trusted for future loads.

Another alternative, if you cannot find a kiln, is to purchase oven-firing clay, a clay body described at the beginning of this chapter.

Casting

The most widely accepted alternative to firing is casting in plaster. While this process is not overly complex for simple forms such as a head, it can be quite complicated for more elaborate forms. Because casting is a much-employed process in sculpture, you might try at a later time to cast your work in both waste-mold and rubber-mold procedures; good books are available with step-by-step instructions (see *References*).

Laminating

Three materials for laminating sculpture are described: Sculpmetal, Pariscraft, and plastic resins. None, it should be noted, are as satisfactory as firing for providing permanence while still maintaining the surface integrity of the work, but each might serve as a viable alternative to leaving the sculpture in its unfired and vulnerable state. (All products are applied to bone dry work; see *Sources of Supply*.)

Sculpmetal is aluminum powder in a resin base. It is applied in a thin layer with a spatula. It will change the texture of your sculpture and add some thickness to it but will produce a hard, waterproof surface. After drying, which usually takes less than an hour, black Kiwi paste shoe polish mixed with a bit of turpentine can be brushed on to darken the crevices and add contrast; the surface can then be buffed with a spoon to bring up the metal finish. In figure 3–11, Sculpmetal has been applied over Pariscraft.

Pariscraft is dry, plaster-saturated gauze, packaged in long strips and cut as needed. Each strip is dipped in water and wrapped around the sculpture. It adheres to many surfaces.

Pariscraft dries and firms in about twenty minutes. More than one layer can be applied if necessary. It is a good idea, however, to begin with only one thickness all over in order to obscure as little as possible of the clay form underneath.

Plastic resins such as polyester resin or epoxy resin, alone, mixed with filler, and/or used with fiberglass, can be applied as a laminate. Resins are mixed with hardeners according to specific directions on the containers. Resins must be applied in a well-ventilated room. In addition, you must wear rubber or disposable plastic gloves and, if extensive work is contemplated, a respirator mask (see *Sources of Supply*).

First, the resin is poured into a disposable container. If you wish, bronze, in powder form, can be added to the resin. Bronze is an expensive product but will create a natural metal patina in the finished piece. The prescribed amount of hardener is added and the mixture is stirred well. There is limited time (which you will determine precisely only when working) for using the material before it becomes hard; therefore, do not mix too much at once.

Rolls of *fiberglass* can be bought from ¼-inch to 12 inches in width. Strips are cut just as with Pariscraft, but instead of water, resin (described above) is applied to the fiberglass strip, and it is then wrapped over the clay form in a single layer. Color can be mixed into the resin.

Fiberglass can also be purchased by the yard in varying sizes. The yard goods, however, tend to ravel in cutting; therefore, rolls are suggested for laminating small sculptures.

Another type of plastic resin, thicker and requiring neither added filler nor fiberglass cloth, is *autobody filler*, purchased in auto supply shops. See page 58 for application procedures.

Keep outer working clothes separate when working with plastics to avoid transporting vapors or glass strands. Your tools can be washed in warm water if you have used epoxy resin and if you do so immediately. Otherwise, use acetone. Polyester resin requires acetone for cleanup. Continue to use the rubber or disposable gloves for cleanup and wash your hands thoroughly with soap and warm water after working and during work if skin contact occurs. Always observe full protective procedures.

PATINATION (COLORING) AND MOUNTING

If your sculpture has been conventionally fired, it will emerge from the kiln a different color than it went in, due to the chemical changes that took place during the extreme heat of firing. That color will depend, of course, on the kind of clay used.

A simple method of patination, one that gives a natural

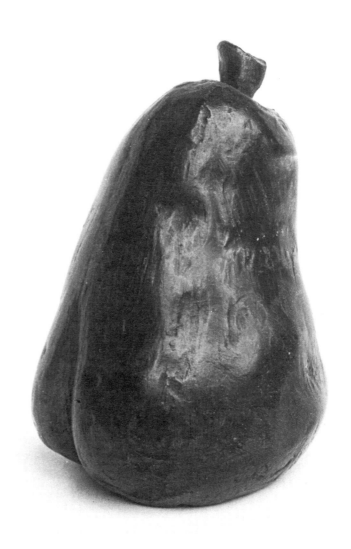

Fig. 2–9. Dark brown Kiwi shoe polish mixed with a small amount of turpentine was applied to the fired clay sculpture as a patina and later buffed. [William Francisco (student), *Pear*; Fired clay. (Photo by Lee Vold).]

wood tone to fired clay sculptures emerging the white, buff, red, or gray of standard clay bodies, is simply to apply shoe polish. Kiwi shoe polish in paste form is suggested. Thin it with turpentine and apply it to the fired piece with a brush, taking care to get into all of the crevices. Dark brown is the most useful color; tones of beige and tan can be added over it as desired. Figures 2–1 and 2–9 illustrate finishes using dark brown Kiwi shoe wax. On the *Duck*, the Kiwi wax was diluted with turpentine to create a duller finish. On the *Pear*, only enough turpentine was added to allow the wax to penetrate the cracks; extra coats of wax were applied as each coat dried to create a hard, shiny finish. When dry, the sculpture was buffed so that a light sheen appeared.

Because the fired clay sculpture will be hollow, the base is likely to be a rim rather than a solid surface. In that case, the sculpture will need to be glued, not drilled, to a suitable base. Refer to Chapter 9 for guidelines for selecting an appropriate base and specific procedures for adhesion by gluing.

EXTENDING THE PROJECT: ART IN HUMAN SERVICE

Because clay is so flexible and handles easily, the potential for using it to create expressive works (of both the inner and external worlds) is unlimited. In this context, the human form is one of the most expressive themes. Making gesture studies in clay, that is, informal, three-dimensional "sketches" of people such as that illustrated in figure 2–10, is a stimulating creative venture. The "sketches" are modeled with spontaneity and with an emphasis on movement and style; little concern is given in this exercise to structural stability or permanence. In this respect, the project is quite different from your other ventures in clay.

Sometimes the addition of color, because of its associations with familiar things in the personal and natural environment, can extend the expressive potential of clay modeling. Use either watercolors or acrylics for coloring. You might spray the finished sculpture with a clear satin polyurethane as a preservative. Try to avoid gloss finishes, which will exaggerate imperfections and tend to dominate the forms; shiny textures, nevertheless, are often enjoyed by individuals doing clay sculptures for the first time.

Acrylic colors should be *mixed* experimentally to obtain more interesting and personal colors than those produced

Fig. 2–10. No attention was given to permanence in this expressive clay "sketch" of a man hollering for his dog. [Unidentified student sculpture. (Photo by Unhjem/ Cavallo).]

directly from the tubes or jars. Colors may also be thinned with water to lessen their tendency to obliterate nuances in modeling.

EXTENDING THE PROJECT: OTHER PROJECTS IN CLAY

The figure gesture studies mentioned above are excellent exercises to prepare you for making a concentrated figure study in clay, using a model. A moderate-size seated or reclining figure is best produced for this long study, as it can be supported by wooden blocks placed as you work. A wooden dowel, temporarily inserted in the torso of the figure, will provide additional support if needed; it is removed at the time of hollowing. Figure 2–11 illustrates an unfired gesture

Fig. 2–11. This seated nude was modeled as a "gesture" study in preparation for a long, concentrated figure study. [Unidentified student sculpture. (Photo by Unhjem/ Cavallo).]

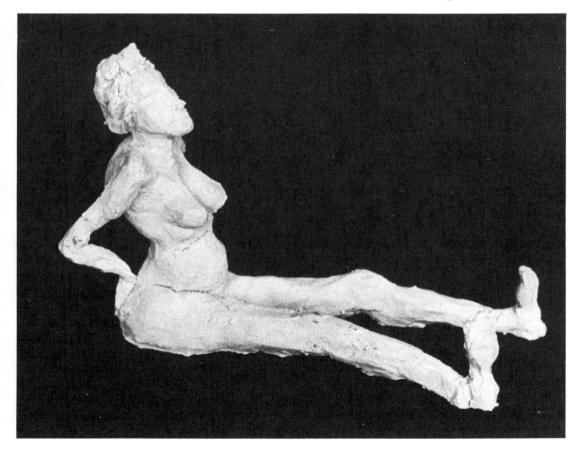

study done by a student as an exercise before embarking on a long study of the model.

Clay is an excellent medium to use for making models for larger pieces or for working out your ideas for works in other media. Plastiline, an oil-base clay (not water-base like kiln-firing clay) does not dry and is especially useful for this purpose.

Large sculptures can also be made in clay and kiln-fired by first cutting the sculpture into sections, then hollowing and scoring the sections for assembly with epoxy resin after firing.

Many useful clay items can be made with sculptural integrity, including pottery, jewelry, wind-chimes, and even lamps. With care and concern for the medium's strengths and weaknesses, you can use clay to accomplish any number of aesthetic objectives.

The Figure in Foil and Pariscraft 3

CREATING the figure in foil and Pariscraft is not complex in either method or materials. Therefore, one week is sufficient to see the project through as described and to begin to get ideas for ways to extend the project at a later time.

THE NATURE OF THE PROJECT

The ability to create three-dimensional figures in action is one most beginning sculptors do not have. Yet, having that artistic ability is valuable if you want to represent and communicate to others your perceptions of the human activities around you. The project described below involves creating a figure or a group of figures engaged in various activities (such as sports, socializing, performances, everyday duties, and so on) and placing the figures in interesting spatial compositions.

From the outset, the efforts of the artist can be devoted more to aesthetics and content than to mastery of materials and techniques in this engaging medium. In addition, the supplies needed are inexpensive and accessible (most are available in the usual household), a situation that tends to minimize the fear of failure.

FOIL AND PARISCRAFT: THE BASIC MEDIA

Aluminum foil, sold for use in the kitchen, is available in two thicknesses: regular and heavy-duty. The regular thickness comes in 12-inch widths and is recommended for this project since a 12-inch square is a viable size to cut for the initial figure pattern. The heavy-duty foil is 18" wide and when cut into a square, will produce a larger figure (18 inches tall) or, when cut in quarters, four very small figures (9 inches tall each). It is suggested that you begin with the

Fig. 3–1. The design of the musical instruments (artifacts), the stance of the figures and their placement on the base are all factors in the success of this group composition. [Walter Tanks, *The Band*; foil and Pariscraft. (Photo by Lee Vold).]

regular 12-inch width and perhaps later, experiment with the greater width. The foil, in either case, must be covered with a firmer material to stabilize the sculpture.

Pariscraft, a coated gauze, is particularly well suited for covering aluminum foil figures. You may be familiar with it in other thicknesses, sizes, and coating substances if you have ever broken an arm or leg and had the limb wrapped in rolls of plaster-coated gauze. For use as an art medium, it is sold in individual rolls or by the carton. When strips are cut from the roll and dipped in water, the plaster is activated and the drying and hardening process begins. The material is odorless, nontoxic, and easily washed off the working surface. It is therefore a convenient product to use in the nonstudio facility. It is also thin enough to conform to the shape of the foil.

CHECKLIST OF TOOLS AND MATERIALS

The equipment mentioned is pictured in figure 3–2:

- Cotton: for forming the head and other areas requiring mass. Use nonsterile rolls (for economy) or cotton balls; toilet tissue or facial tissue can also be used.
- Empty coffee tins: for holding water.
- Scissors: for cutting Pariscraft into strips.
- Small straight pins: for adding artifacts to the figure composition (optional).
- Cardboard: for creating environments or furnishings (optional).
- Hammer

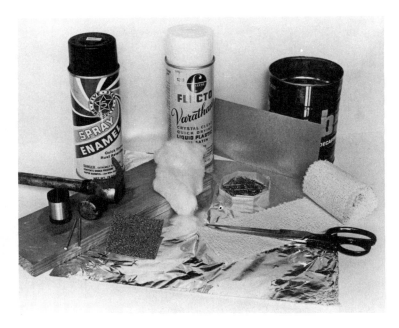

Fig. 3–2. Tools and materials for foil and Pariscraft sculpture. (Photo by Lee Vold).

- Brads: (headless nails) approximately 3 inches long, for securing standing figures to base; use longer or shorter brads according to support needed.
- Thin wire: for wrapping at least one leg of the figure to a supporting nail.
- Wooden bases: small, square, or rectangular, depending on figure composition.
- Sandpaper (assorted grits): for preparing bases
- Spray enamel (black gloss, semigloss, or flat, as desired): for painting bases.
- Kiwi shoe polish in wax form (dark brown suggested): for use as an alternate finish for bases.
- Polyurethane spray, clear or satin: for a protective finish (optional).

PROCEDURES FOR FORMING THE FIGURE

Cut a square of foil (12 by 12 inches) and place it on a flat surface. To form the head, tuck a small amount of cotton just below one corner of the square and wrap and squeeze it

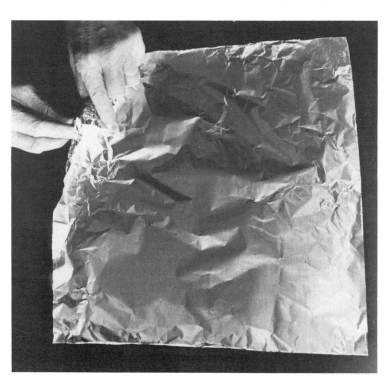

Fig. 3–3. Begin by cutting a square of foil. For the head, wrap cotton in one corner and squeeze it into a ball. (Photo by Lee Vold).

into a ball (figure 3–3). Two small cotton balls, two squares of toilet tissue, or half a facial tissue are the amounts to use to form a head that will be in good proportion to the body. Flatten the foil sheet. Then, beginning at the corner opposite the head, tear from that point to the middle of the square to begin forming legs. The legs will be uneven in length (figure 3–4) due to the configuration of the initial square, but this will be rectified. Again, flatten the foil so that you can see clearly what you are doing. Squeeze the two cut halves into legs (figure 3–5). Fold the foot of the longer leg upward to even the legs; fold the foot of the shorter leg as well to give it more substance. The procedure should result in legs and feet of equal size.

Two large arcs will now remain below the head on either side. Begin about one-third down on each arc and tear horizontally toward the middle of the square to begin forming arms (figure 3–6). Leave enough foil in the center to form the body. Once again, flatten the foil sheet. Now, squeeze the upper portions of the two cut arcs into arms; like the

Fig. 3–4. Starting at the corner opposite the head, tear inwards to the middle of the square to separate the legs. (Photo by Lee Vold).

Fig. 3–5. Squeeze the two cut halves into legs. (Photo by Lee Vold).

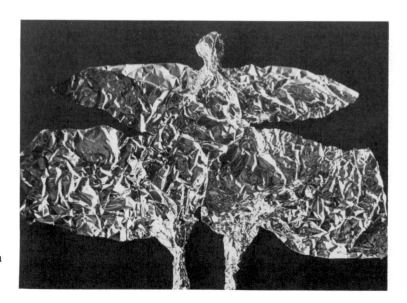

Fig. 3–6. Tear toward the middle of the square to begin forming arms. (Photo by Lee Vold).

legs, they will be uneven in length (figure 3–7). Fold the end of the longer arm inward to even the arms; fold the ends of each arm to form hands.

The remaining foil can be used in several ways. It can be squeezed into the midsection as part of the body or it can be further manipulated into wearing apparel, e.g., skirt, dress, shorts, or pants (figure 3–8). Cotton or tissue can be added and covered over with foil to form breasts, belly, or buttocks.

If longer arms are needed or if a tear occurs, cut a strip of foil and place it across the shoulders (it will look like a shawl); then squeeze it outwards from the neck and shoulders to form arms (figure 3–9). Cut to the length desired. Add extra sheets of foil elsewhere in similar fashion as needed.

When the figure is fully formed, it is ready to be bent into action poses. Remember that bends, twists, and pivots occur *only at the joints* and along the spine. Try many different movements and movement combinations, adjusting the figure at: the neck, the shoulders, the elbows, the wrists, the waist, the hips, the knees, or the ankles. Do not bend the figure along the straight "bones" or you will make snake-like forms, anatomically unrealistic. Practice bending your own body in front of the mirror to see where movement is natural. Move the figure in several ways before selecting a final pose (figure 3–10).

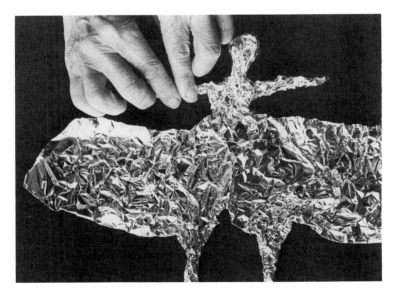

Fig. 3–7. Squeeze the separated upper sections into arms. (Photo by Lee Vold).

Fig. 3–8. The remaining foil can be squeezed into the midsection as part of the body, stuffed with cotton or tissue for fuller anatomy, or shaped into wearing apparel. (Photo by Lee Vold).

Fig. 3–9. "Mending" or extending a form is done by adding strips of foil as needed. (Photo by Lee Vold).

Fig. 3–10. The figure can be moved in many different ways before a final pose is decided upon. (Photo by Lee Vold).

GROUP COMPOSITIONS

Make a second figure and possibly a third to relate specifically to the first. One reason for doing this is to practice making figures while the procedures are fresh in mind. More important, however, is the aesthetic advantage—the increased opportunity to make dynamic designs in space (figures 3–1 and 3–11).

Experiment by manipulating the figures in a variety of attitudes; for example, the figures need not be erect; one or more can be sitting, lying down, falling, kneeling, and so on. They can be engaged in work or play activities; fights or embraces; performances of all kinds (music, theater, dance,

Fig. 3–11. Positioning the figures on different levels can add to the sculpture's vitality. This foil and Pariscraft composition is laminated with Sculpmetal and colored with black Kiwi shoe polish. [Theadora Zacker (student). (Photo by Lee Vold).]

circus acts, gymnastics) or simply walking, talking, eating, or taking out the garbage. The figures may be enhanced by artifacts such as ropes (figure 3–19), tennis rackets, grand pianos, or park benches (figure 3–23). Make artifacts out of foil, cotton, wire, wood, cardboard and so on. Some artifacts are best added directly in Pariscraft, cut in fringes, rope lengths, and many other shapes as in figure 3–20, where Pariscraft strips are laid over wire to create a scarf waving in the air.

MOUNTING AND FINISHING

Before finishing your work you will want to select a base and tentatively position the single figure or group composition (see figure 3–12).

Fig. 3–12. Two foil figures are tentatively mounted to test their relationship to one another and to the base. [Student composition. (Photo by Unhjem/Cavallo).]

Applying the Pariscraft

The Pariscraft lamination should begin after the entire figure composition has been formed and planned as to its position on the base. Additional bends in the figures can be made after the Pariscraft has been applied, but only for a limited period as setting begins about twenty minutes after the material is dipped in water.

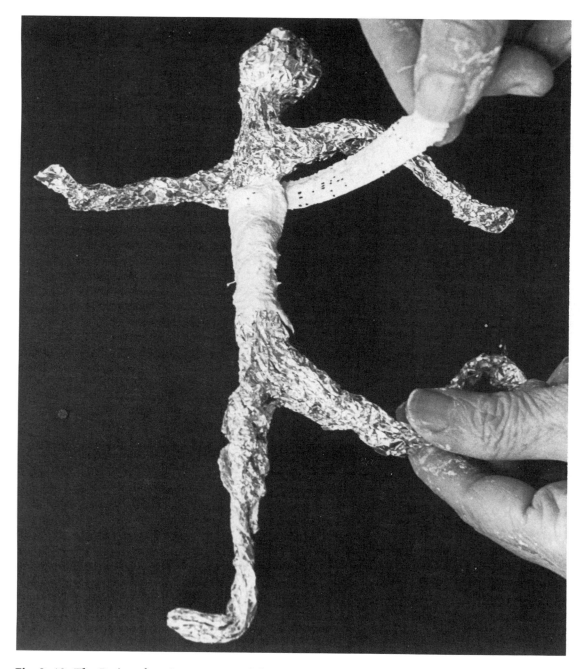

Fig. 3–13. The Pariscraft strips are cut and dipped lightly into water, then wrapped around the form. (Photo by Lee Vold).

Cut strips of the dry Pariscraft to whatever width and length seem manageable. A narrow width, about ¼ inch is suggested in starting out, as the thin strip will be easier to control. Dip the strips lightly, one at a time, in a can of water and apply around the form (figure 3–13). Cover all of the sculpture except for the lower portion of the standing leg or legs; the reason for this will be given below. One layer is sufficient to create a firm surface. More than that may add bulk and alter the forms. Control the application of strips so that unintentional lumps do not appear. Try extending the Pariscraft beyond the figure in various places to create lines that will enliven your figure, such as costuming and hair (figure 3–14).

Fig. 3–14. The Pariscraft can be applied directly to make costuming and hair. [Unidentified student sculpture. (Photo by Lee Vold).]

Preparing the Base

The relationship of base to sculpture must always be an integral one; the base must "belong." It should set off the sculpture from its surrounding environment and should enhance, not detract, from the total conception. A relatively thin base is best suited to the foil figure composition, as the figures tend to be linear in form; a thick base could be overwhelming.

Select the appropriate size and shape for the base. Cut the edges of the base *squarely* (not irregularly) to size. Sand the surface and sides and remove all traces of grit and dust. It can then be spraypainted (black is recommended but not legislated), waxes (dark brown Kiwi shoe polish in paste form makes a good finish), or oiled (with linseed oil mixed half and half with turpentine). Refer to Chapter 9 for further guidelines on base selection and preparation.

Mounting the Figure

Small nails are adequate to support seated or prone figures, with patches of Pariscraft applied to cover the nail-heads.

If the figure is to stand erect, do not completely laminate the standing leg with Pariscraft when you cover the rest of the figure. That leg (or legs), in order to support the standing figure, should first be wrapped with wire around a nail that has been driven into your prepared base. Use a long brad; nail it securely to the base and wire the foil figure to it just above or below the knee, depending on the pose (figures 3–15 and 3–16). Then apply a strip of Pariscraft to cover the leg, wire, and nail.

Protective Spray

The sculpture is essentially "finished" after the Pariscraft is applied and it is mounted. To protect the figures from dust and grease and at the same time add a slightly reflective surface, spray them with a clear satin or gloss polyurethane.

Color

In general, the form and movement of the figures in action show up most forcefully when the sculpture is left an unpainted white. The use of color is, of course, a matter of personal preference. One must only be aware that sculptural form presents an entirely different visual impact when col-

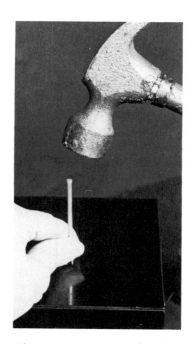

Fig. 3–15. Hammer a brad into the prepared base to support the figure. (Photo by Lee Vold).

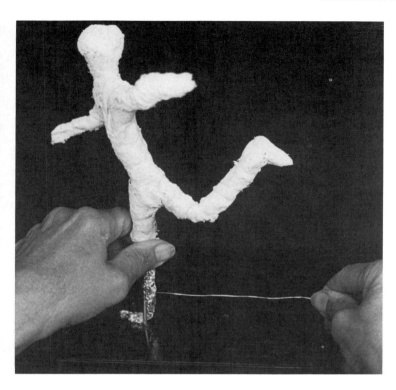

Fig. 3–16. Wire the figure to the nail. Afterwards, cover the supporting leg with a strip of Pariscraft. (Photo by Lee Vold).

oring is added. To color the finished Pariscraft figures, use watercolors or acrylics diluted with water.

EXTENDING THE PROJECT: OTHER POSSIBILITIES

Two options for coating the sculpture and some suggestions for more ambitious constructions are described below to make you aware of some effects that may enhance your ideas.

Coating with Autobody Filler

Autobody filler is a plastic resin used to repair dents in automobiles. It is available in auto stores and body shops. It is not as pleasant to use as Pariscraft as it emits strong vapors. You must work in a well-ventilated area and wear disposable gloves. The product produces a hard, durable finish that can be ground smooth with hand files or left roughly textured. The hardener determines the color of the resin; there are two choices: brown and black.

To use autobody filler, follow these procedures:

1. Work on a clean, flat, portable disposable board.
2. Remove one heaping spatula-full of filler from the can (spatula width, approximately 1½ inches) and place it on your board. Close the lid of the can.
3. Squeeze a thin ribbon of filler once across the diameter of your mound (larger amounts will create larger diameters). Mix well but quickly.
4. Using a flat blade, a small flexible Squeegie, or a household knife, apply the mix, swirling or daubing to obtain the texture you want as you apply it.
5. You must experiment to see how much time you have to work before the mix hardens. Use small amounts until this is determined. Repeat the mixing processes until the sculpture is laminated.

One layer of resin is sufficient. Never put a tool covered with particles of mix back into the can, as this will eventually cause the whole can to set. Instead, use your spatula only for extracting filler; use another tool for adding hardener and stirring. In figure 8–16, wax is coated with autobody filler.

Coating with Sculpmetal

Sculpmetal is plastic mixed with aluminum powders and is available in sculpture supply stores. It is applied directly from the can and does not require the addition of hardener. It is therefore less cumbersome to use than autobody filler but is also less strong. Add no more than ¼ inch of Sculpmetal at a time, allowing that to air dry before the next layer is applied. Again, work in a well-ventilated area. Figure 3–11 illustrates a foil figure covered first with Pariscraft, then with Sculpmetal. The finish is achieved with black Kiwi paste wax.

Making More Ambitious Constructions

You can create larger and more complex structures with the use of Pariscraft, using other materials as the foundation. While it is beyond the intended scope of this section to describe such constructions, you should be aware that materials such as wire, chicken wire, and wire screening or mesh can be used as supports for Pariscraft figures, as in the two illustrations opposite.

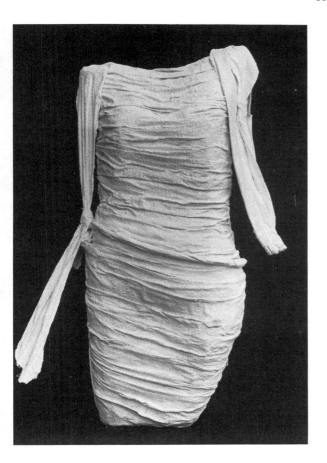

Figure 3–17 shows a torso in which Pariscraft was applied over chicken wire. In figure 3–18 Pariscraft was applied over wire mesh. Note that in both instances the draping quality of Pariscraft is used to advantage. Plaster of Paris should be applied to the Pariscraft to add substance: prepare as described on page 98; however, make only a small quantity at a time (perhaps a cupful) and do not stir. Put cold water in a separate cup and brush the area to be coated. This will moisten your sculpture so that the fresh plaster will adhere. You can use a flat-bladed knife or plastic modeling tool to apply the plaster to your piece.

The foil and Pariscraft project can be extended in a variety of ways, some of which you may invent by incorporating objects lying about your work place. Figures 3–19 (a man

Fig. 3–17. *Above left:* **Pariscraft was applied over chicken wire, which was first cut and shaped. [Theadora Zacker,** *Judith.* **(Photo by Lee Vold).]**

Fig. 3–18. *Above right:* **Pariscraft was applied over wire mesh supported by aluminum wire, with portions built up using foil. [Sam Pepperman,** *Seated Figure.* **(Photo by Lee Vold).]**

Fig. 3–19. Artifacts such as wire or rope add elements of spontaneity as well as design to the action figure. [Paul Barbier, *Runner*. (Photo by Lee Vold).]

crossing the finish line) and 3–20 (a swirling dancer) illustrate animated compositions using wire.

EXTENDING THE PROJECT: ART IN HUMAN SERVICE

It is easy to see the expressive potential of this project. Individuals can portray much about their own body image and the way in which they view others by the style and actions of their foil figures. Evocative group compositions, in this case by students, are illustrated in figures 3–21 to 3–23: a beer-drinking man watching television, a family sitting together on a bench, and a mother and child seated under a tree. Each composition strikes a mood, and although the groupings may convey familiar circumstances, they also project emotional associations to the viewer. Because human figures in various surroundings are relatively easy to produce in foil and Pariscraft, the project can be an initial step in

Fig. 3–20. Wire was used as a frame to support the scarf, with strips of Pariscraft applied as drapery. The movement of this dancer arrested in a turn is vividly described by the circular swirls. [Arlene Beckman (student). (Photo by Unhjem/Cavallo).]

generating provocative and productive discussion about how one feels in these situations. In this context, it is recommended that participants create group compositions rather than single figures to explore more fully the interrelationship of the people portrayed.

The addition of color will extend the expressive possibilities. Choosing colors is important when using art in human service for many reasons: colors have emotional significance; color adds the ingredient of "play," which can be liberating; and having to choose what colors to use (like making personal decisions of any kind) can be beneficial in some circumstances.

Fig. 3–21. William Francisco, *Superbowl.* (Photo by Lee Vold).

Fig. 3–22. *Seated Family.* [Unidentified student composition on painted wood platforms. (Photo by Unhjem/ Cavallo).]

Fig. 3–23. *Mother and Child*; Wooden sticks and found objects added. [Geralyn Clare (student). (Photo by Unhjem/ Cavallo).]

4 Found-Object Sculpture

IF your sculpture proceeds easily, which might happen if the objects are already on hand or are particularly easy to assemble, then you will not need a week to produce one sculpture. You may, in that case, use the remaining time to make a different kind of found-object sculpture: a relief (wall piece), a hanging mobile, or a standing kinetic sculpture (mounted upright but capable of being set in motion). Once you understand the mechanics of assembling articles into a cohesive sculpture, you can create foundation structures in many different ways.

THE NATURE OF THE PROJECT

Creating found-object sculpture involves what the name suggests: finding objects and making sculptures out of them. This project is an excellent one for beginning sculptors, as the opportunity for making aesthetic decisions (the heart of art-making) is continuous from beginning to end, while the necessity to master materials is much less a critical factor than in other three-dimensional media.

Found-object sculpture is highly improvisational. Instructions for the project are minimal and flexible in nature, not step by step, and are offered as a menu of possibilities from which you can choose. Guidelines are given as to what things might be used for your sculptures as well as various methods for assembling them. All of the guidelines have aesthetic objectives that must not be overlooked in the flurry of gathering and grouping objects.

FINDING OBJECTS FOR THE PROJECT

Objects for "finding" are literally everywhere. Below are some suggestions for items to be found outdoors, followed by items generally found indoors. Readers will undoubtedly

Fig. 4–1. In found-object sculpture, space is organized by relating lines, shapes, and mass to create a dynamic interplay. [Amy Robinson (student). (Photo by Lee Vold).]

think of other artifacts that are both aesthetically sound and mechanically feasible as their projects get underway.

Outdoor Found Objects

- Nature's debris: branches, roots, bark, stones, bones, feathers
- Construction materials: roofing, wire mesh, concrete fragments, wire, wood, plastics
- Human debris: broken garden tools, bicycle parts, tin cans, cigarette boxes, wrappers, garden gloves, hose parts, flower containers, machinery parts

Indoor Found Objects

- Hardware: bolts, nuts, washers, flanges, brackets, hooks, hinges, screws, nails, stakes
- Broken toys
- Clothing fragments and fabric scraps, cord, rope, ribbon, shoelaces, thread
- Kitchen utensils
- Broken or obsolete appliance parts
- Electrical, machine, plumbing, and computer parts
- Cartons, packaging materials: cardboard, corrugated paper, Styrofoam
- Old costume jewelry

CHECKLIST OF TOOLS AND MATERIALS

The tools and connective materials needed for the sculpture will depend on the nature of the objects to be assembled. Those listed below (figure 4–2) are universal enough to enable you to consider a wide spectrum of found objects for your compositions. It is wise to regard all of the tools and materials as *optional* rather than necessary until the objects for the sculpture are collected and the tasks of cutting, bonding, and mounting become clear.

- ¼-inch or ⅜-inch drill with assorted bits (the bit size determines the diameter of the hole)
- Cutting shears
- Wire snips
- Saw
- Soldering iron
- Hammer and nails
- Pliers or vise grips
- Knife
- Supporting base (not shown)
- Masking tape and gray duct tape
- Cord and wrapping wire
- White glue and contact cement
- Five-minute Epoxy resin and hardener
- Flat black and flat dark-brown spray enamel

CRITERIA FOR SELECTING OBJECTS

The objects to be found for making sculptures are indeed plentiful, but because of the immense variety of items available, it may be tempting to include things simply because they are interesting in and of themselves. It is a good thing to be intrigued by the shape and form of objects (in fact, it is actually a necessary first step) but it is easy to be seduced by an enchanting variety of collected materials without seeing how they can be integrated into sculpture. You may want to hold onto interesting objects for future use; however, simply assembling single objects and joining them will result in a jumble of unintegrated forms that will ultimately produce not a sculpture but an exhibition of collected items. To keep this from happening, certain criteria for selection are set forth to help you avoid the pitfall of becoming more a collector fascinated with things than an artist interested in designing a single work.

Fig. 4–2. Tools and materials for found-object sculpture. (Photo by Lee Vold).

Obviously, the criteria for selection may be modified according to your own ideas for specific works. However, certain broad features for an aesthetically sound assemblage can be described. It should be noted that most of your decisions will in the long run be intuitive; that is, you will have a gut feeling of what works and what does not work. Nevertheless, in the beginning, it is important to consider formal aesthetic concepts so that you can address the issue of why something is or is not working and how a visual problem might be solved.

Organization

Attention must be given to the outer and inner line formations that give movement and vitality to the sculpture. Movement patterns may be curved, angular, geometric, and so on. The line formations are the contours of the sculpture; for example, what is seen in the silhouette (figure 4–3).

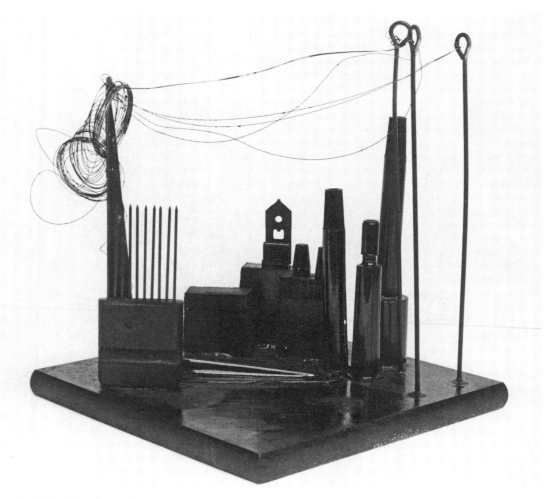

Fig. 4–3. The line formations or contours are what give movement and vitality to the sculpture. [Peggy Loeffelman (student). (Photo by Lee Vold).]

In addition to concern about line, attention must be given to the relationship of *forms* and *shapes*, that is, organizing forms of different mass (thin, thick, concave, convex, open and airy, closed and dense) and shapes of different widths, depths, and heights to achieve a dynamic interplay between them (see figure 4–1). Also, when there are many diverse shapes and changing linear directions in the composition, a massive form can provide visual stability, as in the cylindrical and solid circular forms in figure 4–1.

Finally, attention must be paid to color relationships. In found-object sculpture, many disparate objects might be placed together because the lines, forms, and shapes make aesthetic sense, but the sharply different colors might so intrude upon the composition that cohesiveness is lost. In such cases, it is wise to spray the sculpture some unifying color so that the impact of the total composition will prevail.

Transformation

For found objects to "work" as the components of a sculpture, they must in some way be transformed from their form and function as objects to their place as part of a sculptural composition. For example, it might be amusing to use your uncle's baseball cap in a sculpture, but it will be only a short-lived curiosity if the cap is not transformed into a form that makes sense within the piece. The viewer might recognize real objects used in the sculpture, as in figure 4–4, a playful assemblage of very recognizable items, but the objects should be transformed in such a way that their primary reality is no longer the function they served in their first life but the role they play in their second life as part of your sculpture. Picasso's *Baboon and Young*, a sculpture that incorporates a toy car and a beach ball in the composition, illustrates this point effectively (figure 4–5). Two student sculptures utilizing household hardware also exemplify the transformation process (figures 4–6 and 4–7).

Aesthetic Harmony

Aesthetic harmony refers to the need for a kind of visual logic to be present in the sculpture. For one example, instead of a chaotic display of textures there will exist a visually logical relationship between smooth and rough forms. Any number of examples could be given, yet none should be considered rules, only factors to be considered.

Pointing out the need for "visual logic" or aesthetic harmony is not meant to indicate that the items themselves must be logically related; a tennis ball can certainly be placed next to an umbrella. Aesthetic harmony implies, rather, that the full visual vocabulary of sculpture should be considered as you make your selection of objects and arrange them in interrelationship. "Does it work?" you might ask yourself. If it doesn't, what's wrong?

Listed below are some of the aesthetic components that you might think about. You may find that problems result from there being too much or too little of one or more of these components, or too much or too little contrast between

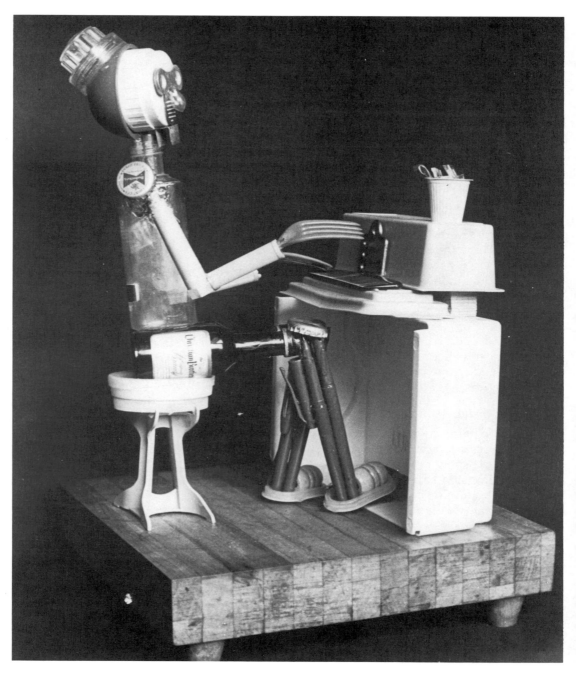

Fig. 4–4. Objects used in found-object sculpture may be very recognizable, but are transformed with playful logic in this ambitious student composition. [Joyce Ann Van Dyke, student. *Jazz Man.* (Photo by Lee Vold).]

Fig. 4–5. The successful transformation of found objects—an oil can, a beach ball and a toy car—into sculptural form constitutes a change in the objects' primary identity from the uses they served in their first life to their role as an integral part of the sculptural composition. [Pablo Picasso, *Baboon and Young* (1951); Bronze (cast 1955), found objects, 21″ high, 13¼″ × 6⅞″ at base. Collection, The Museum of Modern Art, New York. Mrs. Simon Guggenheim Fund.]

Fig. 4–6. The viewer recognizes first the figure of the guitarist with his/her guitar and only secondarily, the hardware out of which it is made. Such lively transformation of objects constitutes both the success and the reward of found-object sculpture. [Unidentified student sculpture. (Photo by Unhjem/Cavallo).]

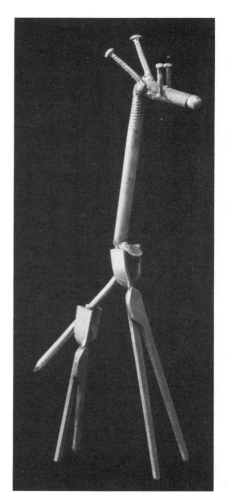

Fig. 4–7. The nails and tongs provided the idea and the materials for this giraffe and then became secondary, only a curiosity, in the final sculpture. [Susan Balacich (student). (Photo by Unhjem/Cavallo).]

and among the various elements of the composition:

- Light and shade
- High points and low points
- Concavities and convexities (depressions and mounds)
- Massiveness and delicateness
- Contours: internal and external
- Balance
- Rhythm, fluidity of lines
- Design: symmetry, asymmetry, repetition; central and peripheral forms; geometric, ameboid, organic forms
- Texture
- Stylistic consistency
- Cohesiveness, coordination, integration

Structural Stability

Stability in this context refers to whether or not the objects selected can be adequately attached with the available tools and materials. For example, a granite rock cannot be drilled without an expensive drill and tungsten carbide bits, and although the concept of holding the rock aloft between two branches might be an excellent one, the task of making it structurally stable would be challenging in a modestly equipped studio (though still not impossible by any means). In any case, the choice of objects should include considerations of weight, gravity, adhesion (to the base and to other objects), and physical balance.

PROCEDURES FOR FOUND-OBJECT CONSTRUCTIONS

The Base

Bases on which the sculptures are attached should be substantial enough to set off the sculpture properly. For example, heavy metal objects require a base that is sturdy enough to stabilize the piece both physically and visually. Lighter materials require a thinner base so as not to overwhelm the interrelating forms. Bases must, of course, be level and not "tippy."

Some sculptures might be more effective as reliefs, in

which case the base will be used to support the sculpture vertically against a wall instead of upright on a table or stand. The decision to make the sculpture a relief might not be made at the outset. Figure 4–8 is a sculpture mounted as a relief, though it was originally constructed upright as shown in figure 4–1. In any case, the base should be integrated into the sculptural composition from the very beginning, utilized as the foundation upon which objects are manipulated and

Fig. 4–8. A found-object sculpture is mounted as a relief, though it was originally constructed upright. [Matty Szymanski, student. (Photo by Lee Vold).]

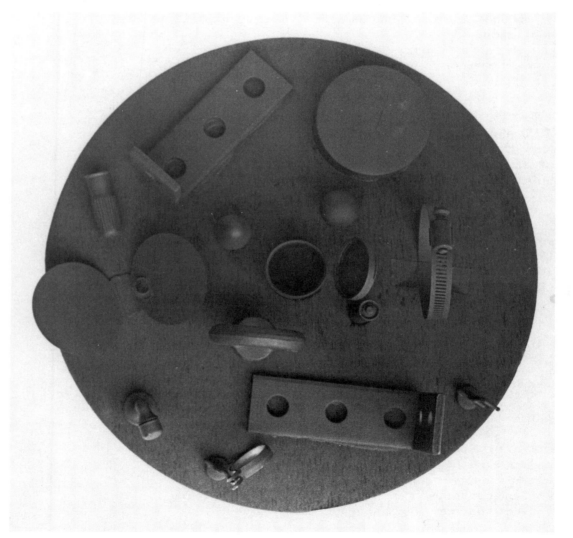

arranged. When the sculpture is completed, the total composition usually becomes more unified if the base is spray-painted the same color as the found-objects.

Temporary Stabilization

When objects have been collected and are ready for assembling into a composition, you face the problem of temporarily balancing the objects to test their visual "rightness" in relation to other objects. To see if relationships "work," you have to let go of the objects after they are placed, and step far enough back to see the impact of the forms in space. The sculpture must also be seen not only frontally but from all sides, and you cannot see how other sides will work without turning the sculpture or moving around it. Gray duct tape is useful for this temporary adhesion as it is strong, sticks well to many types of surfaces, and is easily removed and replaced elsewhere. Larger items can be temporarily supported by rocks, sandbags, cord, or wire.

Permanent Stabilization

Permanent bonding or binding can be made by using any of the materials listed, either alone or in combination. Additionally, there are other products on the market for creating adhesion that you might find equally good and even better for certain purposes. Holes can be drilled into objects to allow two items to be tied together. The natural holes and crevices that occur in objects are also good places for tying.

Aesthetic decisions might be made on the basis of the various devices used to connect one part to another. This is especially so when connecting objects which permit physical movement of the assembled pieces. Parts can be made to move by natural air currents, by fans, or by hand manipulation.

Painting

If parts have been bonded, the bonding agent should be thoroughly dry before painting; if tied, the knots should be buried or covered unless intended to be part of the sculptural form. Nails, staples, and other hardware should be neatly and securely fastened. The sculpture is enhanced when it emerges as unencumbered as possible by the practicalities of its assemblage.

Spray Painting

Such connective materials as masking tape, cord, and wire can be integrated into your sculpture as textures by spray painting the entire composition a single tone when the assembing process is completed. Flat black or flat brown are the recommended choices for spray painting, because the disparity of surface textures that usually appears when found objects are assembled will not be further accentuated by the light reflections that would occur with the use of either a light color or a gloss black or brown.

If color is integral to your composition, use it, of course, according to your concept. However, as stated, allowing the natural colors of the found objects to remain as they are can hinder the "transformation" of separate objects into a single integrated sculpture. When sprayed a single flat black or brown, the various textures will come through as different tones, yet enough integration will be accomplished to allow the sculpture to be seen as a unit.

If plastic packaging material such as Styrofoam is used in the sculpture, latex paint should be brushed on, as spray paint will dissolve it. Partially dissolved Styrofoam might be incorporated, however, as an interesting object within your composition. Always spray paint in a well-ventilated area.

FREEDOM AND LIMITATION

Described at various points in this chapter are what might be termed the freedom and limitations of working in an art medium. The opposing forces of freedom and limitation are present in most art experiences but seem particularly obvious in found-object sculpture: the freedom to select from a wide assortment of existing objects contrasts with the limitations imposed by the need to organize lines, forms, shape, and color; to transform objects into sculptural components; to achieve aesthetic harmony; and finally, to render the work structurally stable. It is important to take note of these opposing forces, as they account for much of the tension and excitement in art-making.

Accepting the theoretical validity of the concept that a contrast between freedom and limitation exists in art-making can have practical implications. For example, the need to channel freedom into some kind of structure can inspire

thematic content, as in figure 4–9, where a man is put together with a confusion of screws, nuts, and bolts. Confusion
about man's nature is implied in this assortment of hardware
designed to hold things together.

Recognizing that there are physical restrictions and limitations that will always be imposed upon the development
of your ideas may relieve some of the frustrations you might
feel as you set about completing the sculpture with the tools
and materials at hand. Such recognition may help get you
through difficult sessions when the exhuberance of creation
has given way to the more mundane tasks of construction
and finishing.

EXTENDING THE PROJECT IN OUTDOOR SETTINGS

A walk in the woods is an ideal place to find stimulation
for constructing sculptures. Do not limit yourself to objects
that can be brought in and assembled. Expand your visual
selections to include anything that has aesthetic components that appeal to you. These might include cloud formations, tree branches, birds flying and alighting, rocks and
boulders, mountain ranges, fish in a pond, joggers, bicyclists,
and so on. The recognition of aesthetically pleasing forms,
whether or not they can physically be taken in and assembled, is often sufficient to bring them into your consciousness as part of your arsenal of forms, to be summoned forth
at some moment when you are actively solving a sculptural
problem.

For more immediate application, a walk in the woods
can be used to collect branches that have evocative formations. The branches can be mounted individually or in combination; they can be collected and organized with human-
istic content in mind or as abstract drawings in space. Branches
can be combined with taut string formations to add tension
to the compositions.

Because found objects are out there for the finding and
collecting (if they don't belong to somebody else), the project
of creating sculptures from them should generate ideas, not
only for the project at hand but for your future work in other
media as well. Selection is a major aspect of art-making, and
the more experience you have in making artistic selections,
the closer you will come to producing from your own personal vision.

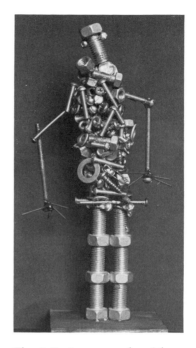

Fig. 4–9. A man made with
nuts, bolts, and other mechanical pinnings is a good
illustration of theme and
content combined. [Stephen
Issler (student). (Photo by Lee
Vold).]

5 Fabricating Wire Sculpture

1 WEEK

THE tools and materials for this project are not difficult to manipulate and, in fact, lend themselves admirably to experimentation. The chances are good that you will be pleased with what you can produce in the one-week time frame.

Fabricating wire sculpture in linear formations can be considered a kind of drawing in space. The wire is "drawn" as the *contours* of a three-dimensional form, and the viewer fills in the masses by imaginative association. Because the viewer, in effect, completes the process of seeing mass where there is only contour, the medium can stimulate a uniquely playful interaction between artist and viewer. In figure 5–1, for example, the viewer is drawn to the artist's perception of two people in conversation by the simple but highly stylized profile lines.

WHY WIRE?

Working in wire is an excellent exercise for the beginning sculptor, in the same way that learning to write journalistically might be for the creative writer. The process forces a simplicity of line and statement and at the same time necessitates well-crafted execution: the lines in their linear sweep must not be unintentionally bent or ragged or they will lose their forcefulness; the connections must hold, yet not be so obvious as to interfere with the visual impact of the "drawing" in space.

Wire is a permanent material and no other steps are required after fabrication to make it durable, though the piece must, of course, be mounted in a manner that holds it firmly in place. Wire is also available in a wide variety of styles and types.

A wire sculpture by Alexander Calder (figure 5–2) and

several student works (figures 5–4 to 5–7), together reveal something about both the fun and the feasibility of working with wire. As you read through this chapter, refer to these illustrations, as well as to figures 5–9 through 5–14 to see the various ways in which the wires were connected and mounted.

Fig. 5–1. The contours of the wire create a drawing in space; the viewer fills in the masses. [Stephen Issler (student); *The Couple*. (Photo by Lee Vold).]

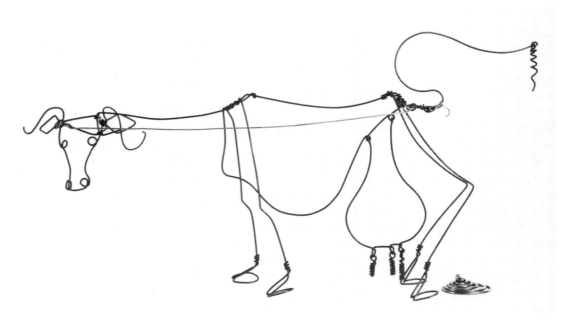

Fig. 5–2. Some of the fun and feasibility of working with wire is revealed in this composition and in student works illustrated throughout this chapter. [Alexander Calder, *Cow* (1929); Wire construction, 6½" × 16". Collection, The Museum of Modern Art, New York. Gift of Edward M. M. Warburg.]

THE BASIC MEDIUM

Wire comes in a variety of widths and weights. You can begin with the idea and try to find wire for it; alternatively, you might look at several kinds of wire and get your ideas from the materials on display. Rolls of galvanized steel, copper, or brass wire are sold at the hardware store. It may also be intriguing to find wire in your own home or neighborhood and get some of your ideas from what turns up there. Clothes hangers are difficult to bend with precision but can be used if cuts and bends are carefully controlled—bent around a rigid form, for example.

Other types of wire to use are strapping wire, aluminum armature wire, thin steel or brass rods, and anything else that can curve, bend, hold its shape, and be joined to other wires and to the base.

CHECKLIST OF TOOLS AND MATERIALS

The equipment mentioned is pictured in figure 5–3:

- Thin wire: for binding; sold in spools and used to connect parts.
- Round-nosed pliers: for forming the wire without creases and for creating hooks that allow wires to be joined without solder.
- Flat-nosed pliers: for creating sharp bends.
- Small table vise: for holding wires to be soldered (optional, not shown).
- Soldering iron: used with solder containing flux; many sculptures will not require soldering, as wires will be joined in other ways (optional).
- Benzomatic jeweler's torch with fine tip: used with solder containing flux; useful for continuing work of a more intricate nature (optional, not shown).
- Wire snips: for cutting thin wire.
- Metal shears: for cutting heavier wire.
- A set of Five-Minute Epoxy resin and hardener (optional, figure 9–14).

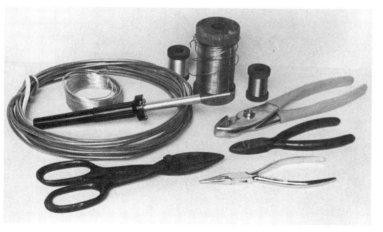

Fig. 5–3. Tools and materials for wire sculpture. (Photo by Lee Vold).

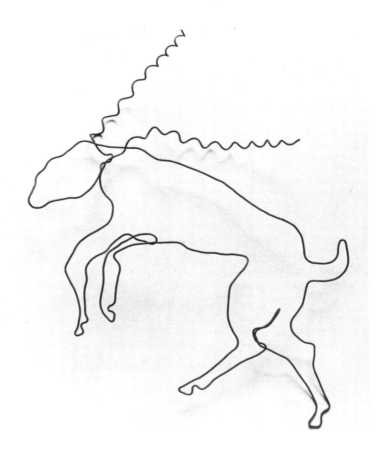

Fig. 5–4. Ingrid Vold (student), *Antelope.* **(Photo by Lee Vold).**

Fig. 5–5. Barbara Lawrence (student), *Elephant.* **(Photo by Lee Vold).**

82

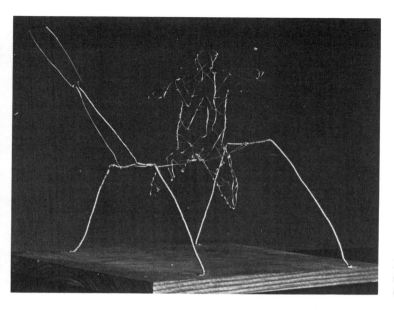

Fig. 5–6. Katherine Deuschel (student), *Horse and Rider*. (*Photo by Lee Vold*).

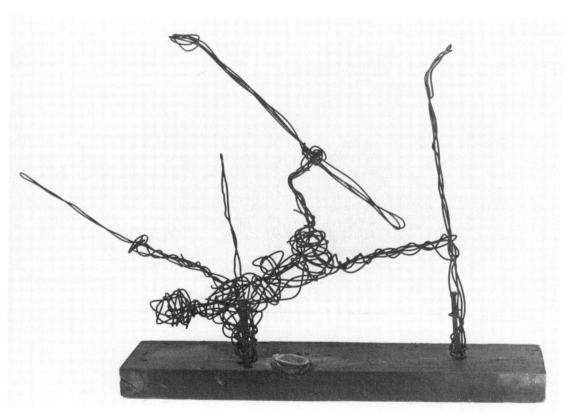

Fig. 5–7. Malik El-amin (student), *Fallen Skier*. (Photo by Lee Vold).

- Staple gun and staples: for mounting (optional, figure 9–14).
- Quarter-inch or ⅜-inch drill with narrow bits: for mounting (optional, figure 9–14).

Most of the tools and supplies needed for making wire sculpture can be purchased in a hardware store or found around the house. Jewelry stores and hobby shops may have a wider selection of wires and pliers. Not all of the tools listed will be needed for the sculpture you do; indeed, very few may be called upon, depending on your choice of materials and design. In any case, securing the parts and mounting the sculpture will vary considerably with each work.

PROCEDURES FOR FORMING AND FINISHING

The first step in making wire sculpture is to select the material to be used. In this as in other projects, the creative process in sculpture can begin in the store or wherever the materials are first seen. The fact that you respond to certain wires and have no interest in others has much to do with your private way of seeing. As you look at and handle the various wires, you may begin to visualize something taking shape. Many things may influence your immediate perceptions: something in nature that you have recently seen; an image that has been settling in your head for some time; even the glimmer of surrounding merchandise if you are shopping in a hardware or plumbing supply shop, or a hobby or art store. Indeed, many of the sights and sensations to which you respond in the present and have responded to in the past will play a part in your initial choice of materials and in your continuous selection of forms during the process of creating.

There is, however, an equal likelihood that you will have no visualization of sculptural forms as you buy or find the wire and look at it, wondering what to make. You may discover what you want to make only after you begin to form the wire into shapes—any shape—just to get started. Whether or not you have something specific in mind, you might begin by securing the wire in one hand with your fingers or with pliers, or in a vise; then simply proceed to bend it (figure 5–8).

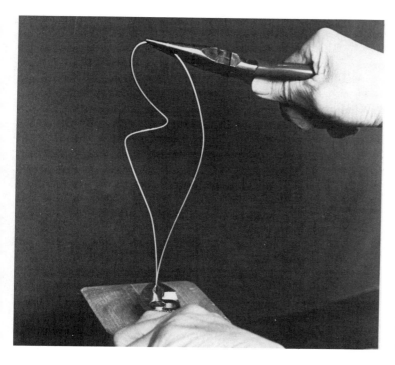

Fig. 5–8. One way to begin is to secure one or both ends of the wire and then proceed to bend the wire improvisationally. (Photo by Lee Vold).

Connecting the Wires

You may be able to make the entire sculpture from a single length of wire, in which case no procedures to connect wires will be necessary, other than securing the sculpture to the base.

If you do need to connect sections of wire, there are various ways to do so:

- Bend a small hook in one end of the wire and a loop in the other (figure 5–9). When the connection is in place, close the hook. Silver wire necklaces and bracelets often have this kind of attachment. You may want to have a moveable sculpture in which the parts can be hooked and unhooked by the viewer.
- Wire the parts together. The connective strands can become part of the sculptural texture, as in figure 5–10.
- Solder the two ends of the connection together. To achieve a good bond, cut the ends so that they are ex-

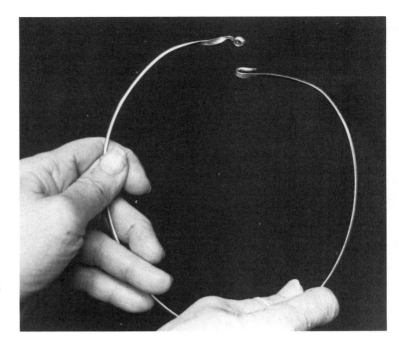

Fig. 5–9. One way to connect wires is to bend a small hook in one end of the wire and a loop in the other. (Photo by Lee Vold).

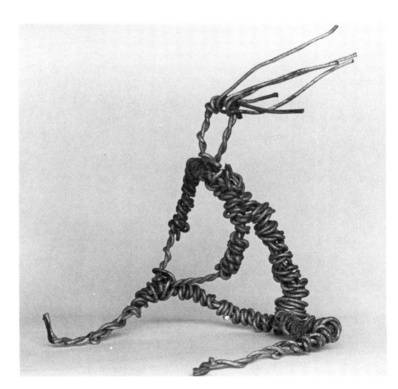

Fig. 5–10. Adding wires in various places can extend the contours of the sculpture and increase the air of spontaneity. [Unidentified student sculpture. (Photo by Lee Vold).]

actly flush; heat the ends, connect while adding a touch of solder to the joint.

STYLE

Wire sculptures may have a wide stylistic range. Forms may be three-dimensional and encompass mass, as in figure 5–11. They can be linear profiles—drawings in space—either figurative (as in figure 5–1) or abstract (as in figure 5–12). They may be amusing, highly stylized compositions, as in

Fig. 5–11. Wire sculptures can have a wide stylistic range. They can be three-dimensional and mass-encompassing, as in this female figure, or linear drawings in space as in figure 5–1. [Margaret Petruchkowich (student). (Photo by Unhjem/Cavallo).]

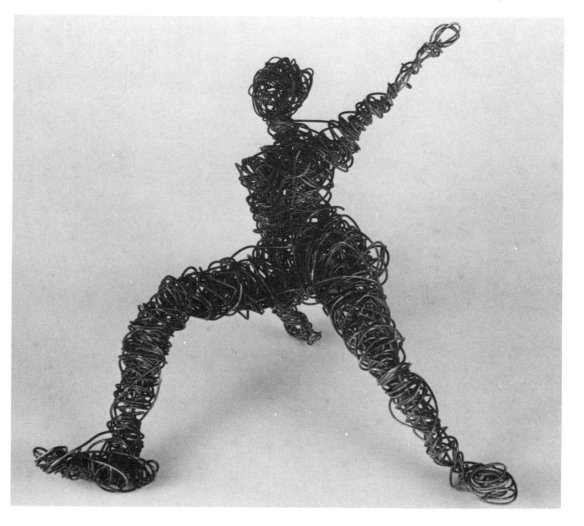

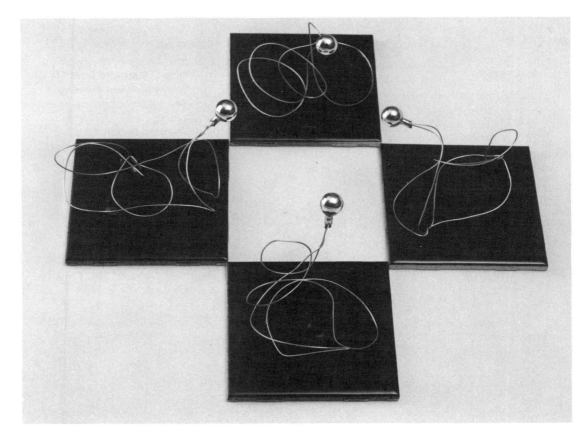

Fig. 5–12. This lively abstract composition in wire, glued onto squares of black ceramic tile, invites viewer participation by its thoughtfully balanced grouping. This viewer sees in it a game with four players, or perhaps children peering into a hole in the ground, or ritual dancers. [Richard Ginelli (student). (Photo by Unhjem/Cavallo).]

figure 5–6, or representations of action, as in figures 5–7 and 5–13. Such compositions afford a liveliness and spontaneity that other materials such as clay, stone, or even foil and Pariscraft are largely unable to provide.

In creating your wire sculptures, just as with other media, try to maximize the qualities that are unique to the wire itself: that is, its extreme linear flexibility; its color and sparkle; the way it receives light and shadow; the ease with which forms can be manipulated and changed; and finally, its lightness and portability, which allow the sculpture to be perched high, set low, and continually turned to be seen from all sides during the lengthy decision-making process. As you begin to actually handle the various wires, you will gradually discover and solve the distinctive challenges that arise.

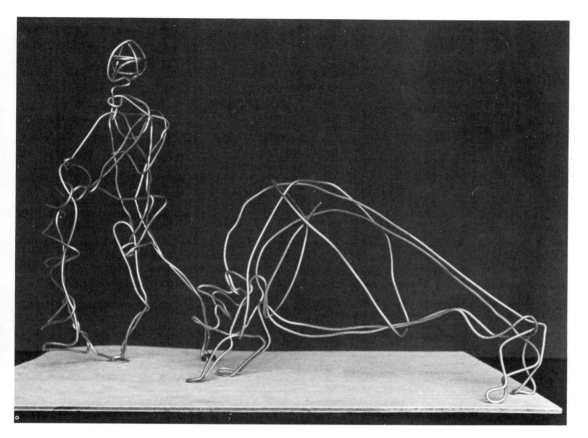

Fig. 5–13. This action composition is in the nature of a three-dimensional "sketch." [Gary Smith (student), *Bull Fighter.* (Photo by Lee Vold).]

MOUNTING

The base should be fully prepared before the sculpture is mounted (see chapter 9 for base preparation and guidelines for mounting). The base must be heavy enough to prevent the wire sculpture from toppling over and also be the right size to complement the design effectively. Depending on the sculpture created—its size, style, and disposition on the base— the following methods of mounting can be considered:

- Nail or staple the wire or wires to the base. Neatly done with the proper nail, brad, or staple, tacking can adequately and aesthetically secure the composition.
- Drill a slender hole deep into the base, keeping it narrow enough to grip the length of wire to be mounted.

Mix a small amount of Five-Minute Epoxy. Coat that section of wire going into the hole and hold until the epoxy has set.

• Solder the sculpture to a metal base. The metal base can then be fixed to a wooden base with contact cement or epoxy resin.

EXTENDING THE PROJECT: MOVING PARTS AND RELIEFS

Wire sculptures can be constructed so that some sections are made to move while the major structure is mounted solidly on a base. A viewer may set it in motion or it can be designed to move gently with natural air currents while mounted. The sculpture can be made as a mobile, in which case it need not be mounted on a base (although a mobile emerging from a base can make an intriguing composition), but instead may be suspended from the ceiling. In making a mobile, you must find the fulcrum, that place where the extended arms of the wire sculpture will balance when suspended. Connecting the wires for a mobile construction can be accomplished in any of the ways previously described.

Wire sculpture can also be made as a relief. The sculpture can be completely formed and then mounted, or it can be created directly on its wall-hung background—a piece of wood, for example. To do this, prepare the surface in advance and hang it on the wall. Then tack the wires in position as you form the composition, making changes as you go along. Life-size sculptures can be made out of wire with comparative ease in this way, since a free-standing support for the composition does not have to be constructed.

EXTENDING THE PROJECT: ART IN HUMAN SERVICE

Wire, in some settings, may be considered too dangerous a material to use because it is sharp and because many of the tools could conceivably cause injury. When this factor is not at issue, the project is a good one because of the potential for producing a successful, durable finished product. Interestingly enough, many individuals who are new to art are quite hesitant about drawing on paper, believing they must be "artists" to be able to "make" anything. Drawing in space with wire, because it is a new experience, has no

Fig. 5–14. This face, composed only of eyes, nose, lips, and hair, demonstrates the expressive possibilities of wire in recreational or rehabilitational settings; the conception is uncomplicated, yet still conveys an expression of animation and surprise. [Arlene Beckman (student). (Photo by Lee Vold).]

similar preconceptions attached to it and is often approached with a positive, explorative attitude. You will note by glancing at the illustrations that wire sculptures need not be elaborately constructed to be effective; simple lines, effectively mounted, can convey a striking image.

Executing simple facial features in wire, as illustrated in figure 5–14, can open an avenue of stimulating discussion concerning one's feelings about self and other people.

6 Carving in Plaster, and Cement and Vermiculite

4 WEEKS

ONE plan is to devote the first two weeks to plaster carving and the next two weeks to carving in cement and vermiculite. A second plan is the reverse. The four-week time period should be structured according to the needs arising out of your specific projects, but each medium has distinctive characteristics to consider: Plaster is softer and less brittle than the cement and vermiculite mix and may prove easier for you as your first carving experience. Plaster lends itself to smooth finishing—a process which takes some time—whereas cement and vermiculite becomes dusty with fine abrasion and is better left rough. Therefore, though more complex to carve, the cement medium may go more quickly. A third alternative is to work on the two projects concurrently.

In this chapter you will explore the processes of mixing and pouring plaster and cement and vermiculite into containers, removing the containers when the mixes have set, and carving the blocks or boulders into finished sculptures. Both plaster and cement and vermiculite are excellent materials to use to approach the experience of carving. Both follow the same general principles, with technical and aesthetic variations particular to each medium.

THE NATURE OF THE MEDIUM: PLASTER

Plaster is a versatile sculptural medium. A gypsum product, it is relatively soft and unresistant to the blade. It has no grain and no impediments. Beginning as a fine white powder, it mixes easily with water into a creamy liquid; it then becomes a semisoft putty, and finally, a solid. Each of these manifestations of plaster's unique identity can be used to advantage in making sculpture, but each has time restrictions, and one must design one's sculptural choreography to meet those limitations.

Because plaster is liquid before becoming solid, it can be

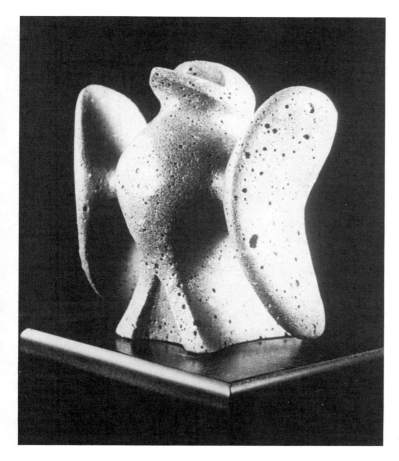

Fig. 6–1. An example of well-defined forms carved in cement and vermiculite, finished and mounted with care. [John Reda (student), *Bird*. (Photo by Unhjem/Cavallo).]

poured into a container or mold, splashed onto or into an existing form, laminated onto cloth or burlap to wrap a form that has been made as an armature (such as chicken wire), and adapted to numerous variations on these themes.

Plaster is the most common material used in making molds for sculpture. Plaster is also used for the casts, although casts are more often made with hydrocal, a stronger gypsum product in the same family. As indicated earlier, this book will not examine the mold-making and casting process, nor will it explore laminating, wrapping, and modeling with plaster. Rather, it will concentrate on the material in its solid state and on its use as a creative medium in carving.

Superfine grade plaster in 5-, 10-, 25-, 50-, or 100-pound

bags can be obtained at art stores or sculpture supply stores; a more porous grade of plaster can be found in paint stores in 5-, 10-, or 25-pound bags and will still be satisfactory for sculpting. Avoid getting moisture in plaster bags, which may make plaster lumpy and unusable.

THE NATURE OF THE MEDIUM: CEMENT AND VERMICULITE

Cement, mixed with sand or aggregates (various stones), is used extensively in building construction and is also a medium for sculpture: the mix is generally either poured into molds taken from clay or plaster models or built up directly onto supported wire lathes. You will be using the cement for carving only, and therefore the casting and building-up process will not be described. For the purpose of the project at hand, a heavy-duty mix is not necessary. What is needed instead is an attractive material that offers permanence without being too difficult to carve. Cement and vermiculite together provide this. The particles of vermiculite (a product used to aerate soil and nurture plants) spread throughout the mix produce a glistening effect similar to the mica found in quartz. This reduces the somewhat dusty quality of pure cement without reducing its solidity.

The cement and vermiculite mix, poured into a container to set, forms a solid, durable, inexpensive medium on which to apply the techniques of carving. It is stronger than plaster, and because of its surface roughness and density, is more closely akin to stone. When cured, it can also be placed outdoors, unlike plaster. The surface is not completely impervious to weather since patterns of pock marks may form with prolonged exposure to the elements. However, these marks might sometimes enhance rather than detract from the texture. The color of the block will be a light gray or an off-white, depending on whether gray or white Portland cement is used. The vermiculite adds gray crystal-like particles to the block. Cement and vermiculite, unlike plaster, takes from one day to several days to set, depending on the size of the block.

Portland cement (cement only, unmixed with sand or aggregates) is found in lumber yards; gray is more readily available than white and is also less expensive, although the product (considering the amount of carving material it produces) is very inexpensive overall. Portland cement is generally sold in 80-pound bags.

Vermiculite is purchased in garden-supply stores in granular form. (It is sold in lumber yards in small chunks as attic insulation, but this product you do *not* want.)

CHECKLIST OF TOOLS AND MATERIALS

The equipment needed is shown in figure 6–2:

- Plastic mixing bowl: 3 quart size or more, depending on the size of the container to be poured (not shown).
- An extra mixing bowl or pail: for catching possible drippings (not shown).
- Steel chisels: for carving the block; at least two, small and medium size; flat-ended are recommended as a start.

Fig. 6–2. Tools and materials for carving plaster and cement and vermiculite. (Photo by Lee Vold).

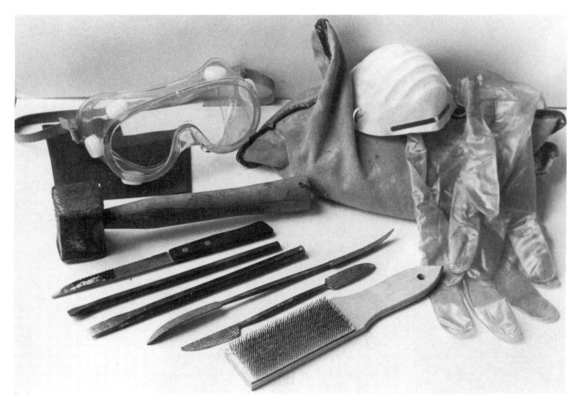

- Steel mallet: for use with chisels in carving the block: 1½-pound for the average woman; 2-pound for the average man. A hammer can be substituted, although it will not perform as well.
- Serrated knife: for push-carving small forms—household variety.
- Metal files and rasps: for modelling forms and smoothing rough areas—a wide variety is available.
- Wire brush: to clear files and rasps of grit.
- Wet/dry Carborundum papers: for smoothing plaster—these are black and are available in coarse, medium, fine, and extra-fine grits.
- Sandbags (2): for supporting work in progress; purchased in sculpture supply houses or made by hand (directions given below).
- Rocks and slivers of wood as needed: for propping work for critical viewing (not shown).
- Sturdy stick: for mixing cement, vermiculite, and water (not shown).
- Disposable gloves (optional): if hand-mixing the cement, vermiculite, and water, contact with the liquid mix can be irritating.
- Dust mask (optional): used when mixing, if you are sensitive to cement dust.
- Goggles (optional): used when carving cement and vermiculite.
- Containers: some suggestions are plastic bags (heavy duty); milk and juice cartons; detergent and bleach bottles; shoe boxes, soap cartons, or other cardboard boxes lined with plastic; plastic cups and deli containers; plastic soft drink bottles with the tops cut off for pouring; any other container that can hold liquid without collapsing and be peeled away when the mix has set.

PREPARING THE PLASTER FORMS

When pouring plaster into a plastic bag, furrows or grooves may be formed that remain when the container is removed. You may decide to work these into your composition (see figures 6–3 and 6–4). When the container is a plastic bottle, the form will be very smooth. You may want to retain portions of those areas in the finished piece; contrasts of smooth and rough texture can be effective in both cement and vermiculite and plaster carving. Words may have been im-

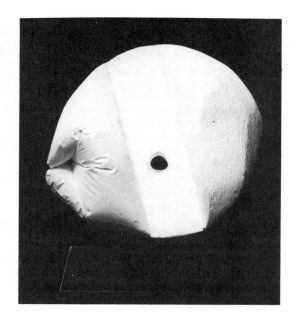 

printed on the container—bleach bottles, for example, have such raised lettering—and you may want to integrate those markings into your sculpture. Any or all of the characteristics or "imperfections" of your container may be utilized in the finished piece. You may indeed decide to do nothing at all with a boulder after its "wrapping" is removed. Figure 6–14 is a product of a pour-and-unwrap procedure.

Fig. 6–3. *Above left*: Furrows or grooves formed by the containers can be worked into the composition. [Unidentified student sculpture. (Photo by Unhjem/Cavallo).]

Fig. 6–4. *Above right:* You may decide to leave the plaster exactly as it was cast in the bag. [Unidentified student conception. (Photo by Unhjem/Cavallo).]

Pouring the Plaster into Plastic Bags

Prepare your plastic bag by checking for holes and then locating a good place to hang or prop the bag after plaster has been poured into it. The plaster will set in a shape that is dependent on the pressure exerted on it—the pressure, for example, of a counter edge or block of wood or mound of clay wedged underneath it—so think about that potential shape as you look around the room for a suitable "setting."

Have someone hold the plastic bag open for you while you pour; if you are alone, hang it inside a pail. In either case, pour over a bowl in case the bag springs a leak. Fill the bag with as much plaster as you think it can bear in weight (or as much as you want to work with). Close the bag tightly with a plastic tie or wire, then hang it up with a wire; or drape it over a counter or some other form that you have chosen and wait until it has set.

Pouring into Rigid Containers

Cardboard boxes and plastic cups, bottles, and jars are suitable as long as they can be peeled away when the plaster sets. If the container is an upright carton, tap it gently after filling so that trapped air bubbles can rise to the top. If it is a long low box, also tap it, but more gently to avoid spillage.

The Plaster Mix

The following procedures for making the plaster mix apply regardless of what type of container is used:

1. Fill the mixing bowl half full with cold tap water.
2. Open the plaster bag to allow wide access at the top and place the bag close to the bowl.
3. Dip your dry hand into the bag and transfer full handfuls of plaster to the bowl by sifting the plaster quickly through your fingers. Work close to the bowl but without touching it.
4. Continue this transfer, distributing the plaster across the bowl. Work quickly but do not jar the bowl.
5. When a mound forms in the middle, let the bowl stand for a few seconds. Then stir. Stir without splashing, with a flat hand, squeezing out lumps as you feel them, until the mix is creamy smooth. Take care not to stir vigorously or air bubbles will form, creating small holes in your solid form. The setting process begins when stirring begins, so work efficiently; the stirring should take no more than two minutes.

Setting

You will have five minutes or so to manipulate the container before the plaster begins to set (this will vary according to the amount of plaster used and the atmosphere). Do not move the container while the plaster is setting.

Setting takes about 20 to 30 minutes, after which the bag will become quite warm. When it cools, the wrapping can be removed and you are ready to carve. If the plaster seems excessively loose as you start to carve, it may need to dry out overnight before you begin.

PREPARING THE CEMENT AND VERMICULITE BLOCKS

Prepare a container. If it is cardboard it must be lined with plastic. Setting time is considerably longer than that for plaster, and the weight of the mix directly against the wet cardboard may cause it to disintegrate.

The procedure for making the cement and vermiculite mix is as follows:

1. Using a stick and a cup, jar, or coffee can as a measure, mix the dry ingredients in a mixing bowl in the following proportions:

    two parts vermiculite
    one part cement

    The total amount used will depend on the size of the container to be filled. If you have not mixed enough, it is all right to mix more and add it; have an empty container handy for overage.
2. Mix well with a sturdy wooden stick. Then add cold water in a slow steady stream while continuing to mix with the stick. A helper who will stir while you add the water may be necessary if the mix is a large one, as the wet ingredients can become quite heavy to manipulate. Avoid pouring large bucketfuls of water at once, as the vermiculite, being lighter than the cement, may rise unmixed to the top.

Pouring the Mixture

When the mix is reasonably smooth throughout and is about the consistency of sour cream, pour it into the containers. Tap the containers gently when full, as you did when filling plaster containers, to bring trapped air bubbles to the surface. Place the cartons where they will not be disturbed for the day or two necessary for setting.

GUIDELINES FOR CARVING

The assumption is that you are working in a nonstudio atmosphere with less than state-of-the-art equipment. If you have more sophisticated equipment than that described here, by all means use it. However, the directions below should enable you to follow through with the carving experience with a minimum of set-up and expenditures.

Supporting the Sculpture with Sandbags

The most convenient and flexible method of supporting your block or boulder is to wedge it onto a sandbag—a canvas bag filled loosely with sand. Your block nestles into the bag, is supported by it, and both your hands are then free for carving. Sandbags can be purchased at sculpture supply stores or made at home.

To make sandbags, begin with a piece of canvas about 22" × 16". Fold it in half. Run seams along all open edges by hand or machine, leaving a pouring area open on the last side. Fill the bag two-thirds full with dry sand (ordinary play or beach sand is suitable). Complete the seam.

Supporting the Sculpture for Critical Viewing

The plaster or the cement and vermiculite form must be propped upright, first one way and then another, to enable you to study what you are starting with. As supports, you can use thin pieces of wood underneath as needed, or you can prop the block against rocks or against your sandbags. If you have the means, you might fill a barrel with sand and use that as a propping-up surface. Use anything that will support the block while still allowing you to see it and turn it.

Visualizing Cuts

As you look at the block, ideas will begin to form about certain cuts you would like to make. Turn the form (or move around it) to see how the changes will work throughout. In the beginning you may not feel very confident at visualizing those consequences. This is understandable, as you still need to gain experience in seeing the effects the cuts will have on other areas; for example, how a deep crevice in one area creates a sharp angular profile in another.

What to Avoid

You may have a tendency, in executing your first carvings, to want to retain the original shape of the boulder or block, and this may lead you to work decoratively, incising the surfaces and creating designs rather than carving. Try to avoid such decorative carving; it probably will result in the creation of separate, unrelated facades in low relief rather than an integrated sculpture in the round.

In this initial carving experience, it is also not advisable to draw predetermined guidelines on the block. It is more adventurous and closer to a direct carving experience to begin by being somewhat guided by the nature of the block. Have a sense of pulling forms out of the block and developing them. Presumably, you had some say in the nature of the block when you chose the container for pouring.

Finally, do not make your forms too complicated. Forms need to have space around them to develop fully. The simpler you make your forms, the more fully each one can be developed and completed.

Some General Working Procedures

- Try to maintain your block in a solidly situated, unmoving position as you work. Do not use your hand to steady the block; instead, secure the work with the sandbags, rocks, sticks, or whatever supports are available to do the job. Your carving hands should remain behind the knife; the only thing in front of the knife should be the sculpture being carved.
- Give yourself a wide berth in making your cuts. Note that the widest point of a round three-dimensional form carved from a block is not on the front or the back of the block but on the sides, as you travel around the block. Allow for this development of the form by beginning your cuts wider than you intend them to be when completed (figure 6–5).
- As a general carving principle, carve *away* from high points. Carving *into* them may result in a high point falling off. There are times when you will find it cumbersome to carve away from the high point and will be forced to carve into it. In that case, protect the high area by first carving down along one side of that area to create an edge. Then when you carve inward, the cut will stop along that edge.

ESTABLISHING FORMS

Whether the forms of your sculpture incline toward abstract or representational is up to you. Abstract work has the advantage of relieving you of the added problem of getting the sculpture to look like something identifiable. In-

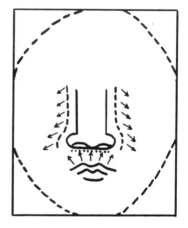

Fig. 6–5. Begin your cuts wider than you intend them to be (indicated by dashed lines). Carve *away* from your high points, not into them (indicated by arrows). If you must carve into a high point, protect it by incising a line with your chisel, creating an edge where the cut will stop (indicated by dotted line).

stead, you can concentrate on the development and relationship of forms. Such an approach is recommended for that reason. However, if you do see something realistic in the stone and can visualize the forms becoming fully developed, by all means represent it. In each situation, however, try not to find a myriad of forms but a few simple ones; then carve them with attention to their contours and how those contours carry around to other parts of the block.

The Relationship of Forms

The process of looking, as examined in chapter 1, is continuous in art-making. So too is the process of selecting. Another continuous process involves relating forms to one another with a view toward aesthetic integrity and stylistic consistency.

What are aesthetic integrity and stylistic consistency? To answer this question, let us look at some examples: a large, voluptuous, well-rounded form alongside slim, convoluted twists and bends is inconsistent in form (figure 6–6). An abstract figure, carved in simplified planes but crowned with a realistically detailed head, lacks aesthetic integrity; it is inconsistent in style (figure 6–7). A sculpture carved with cavernous hollows and massive forms that is then sur-

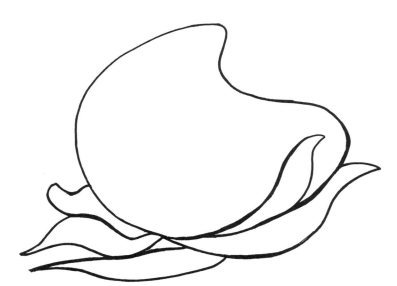

Fig. 6–6. A massive form alongside thin "fragile" spirals is an example of inconsistency in style.

face "decorated" with fussy, intricate lines is inconsistent within its style and will lack the force of an integrated piece (figure 6–8).

An example of beautifully integrated sculptural forms in plaster is seen in Jean Arp's *Human Concretion* (figure 6–9).

Designing Two Separate Forms in Relationship

A good way to go about the study of relating forms, particularly in plaster carving, is to design two completely separate forms in relationship to one another. To do this, you can either pour two separate containers or pour one container and divide it into two parts. The cut can be made with a saw, or the block can be incised in the direction you want and then hit with the mallet and chisel to fragment into two parts. The final sculpture will consist of two forms on one base. The techniques and guidelines for carving and finishing are the same as those described throughout this chapter. The problem of relating forms is still the essential one but is addressed by manipulating two separate masses instead of one. Figures 6–9 and 6–10 are completed examples of this exercise.

Shadows: Lights and Darks

In carving, the element of shadow (lights and darks) is significant. The shadows created as a result of carving your forms can add boldness and strength or accentuate weaknesses in line and design. Note the influence of light and shadow on the sculpture illustrated in figure 6–11.

If you are carving properly, you are turning the sculpture frequently to look, to select, to modify, and to fully establish your forms. As you do this, observe the highlights that are created. Highlights can be smooth and clear or rough and irregular. However highlights and shadows develop in your sculpture, make sure that you recognize their impact on your piece. Remove sharp highlights that interfere or obliterate your forms by rounding the edges that cause them or by blending one form into another. Similarly, accentuate highlights where they can add dramatic depth and interest by cutting more sharply and filing to create crisp edges. Light and shadow, created by the high points and depressions of your carving, should be a strong consideration as you work. The external lighting and placement of your piece are factors

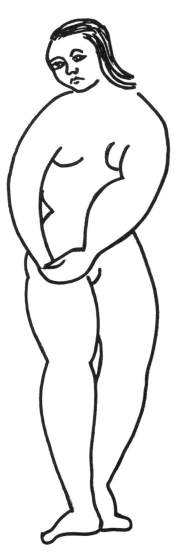

Fig. 6–7. A figure carved in abstract planes but crowned with a realistically detailed head is another example of inconsistency in style.

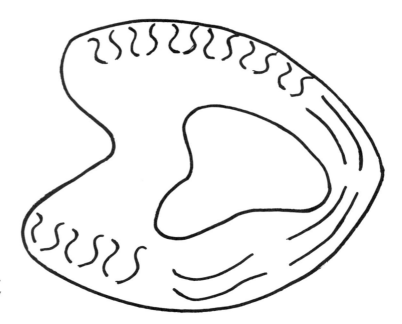

Fig. 6–8. Expansive forms (the hollows and broad surfaces) "decorated" with intricate patterns create a totality that is inconsistent in style.

that will influence light and shadow, but you will be wise to try to direct that influence through critical observation and careful carving as the results can be dramatic.

FINISHING

Let us say that your forms have been reasonably established and you have achieved an overall result that you can live with. It is not perfect, not a pure manifestation of the images floating in your head, not the best you can do. But that, indeed, is what makes artistic creation so tantalizing. Therein lies the stimulus to make other works. Sometimes you might come close to reaching those images—perhaps not often, yet still there is progress. Every time you explore your creative imagery and produce something of its remarkable originality, something that can actually be looked upon and touched, you have progressed. You have done something most people never do in their entire lives, at least consciously. The interplay that has been made between your mind's eye and what appears in the carving is the artistic experience. It is that experience that forms the artistic process, a process that may be the clearest connection it is possible to make between what you do and what you are.

Aesthetic Finishing

Now comes the final refining of your forms. Lumps and scratches, indentations and hollows must be regarded with a brutally critical eye. Do you want them? Are they to remain a part of your finished sculpture? If the answer is "no," if you regard them as imperfections that detract from your design, you might change them by:

- filing the form, reducing it somewhat in size, but keeping the general shape as it is (figure 6–12);
- recarving the form, using the hollows as an impetus for visualizing other, perhaps more exciting forms (figure 6–13).

Fig. 6–9. The two forms that meet and separate in this beautifully integrated plaster sculpture are quite different, yet are consistent in their organic style. [Jean Arp, *Human Concretion* (1949); Replica of original plaster (1935); Cast authorized and approved by artist; Cast stone, 19½″ × 18¾″. Collection, The Museum of Modern Art, New York. Purchase.]

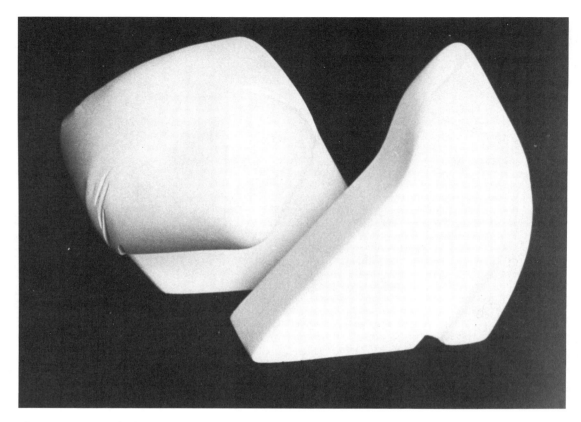

Fig. 6–10. Try to design two completely separate forms, thinking only of their relationship to one another, as in this example. [Karen Sherman (student). (Photo by Lee Vold).]

Frequently, solving the finishing problems serves as a way of making aesthetic discoveries that may not otherwise have been made. Having to define a single form distinctly often results in having to change the surrounding forms as well. Then, as fresh contrasts emerge in depth, mass, line, texture, and shadows, one can carefully select and enlarge upon their impact on the total sculpture.

Filing and Sanding the Plaster Carving

Look carefully at your sculpture and decide what is to be filed and sanded and what is not because you may desire a contrast in texture. You might then smooth some areas but allow others to retain the texture of the carving tools, the files, or the plaster as it emerged from the container.

For the finishing work on your plaster carving, you will need a metal file and wet/dry Carborundum papers. Use the

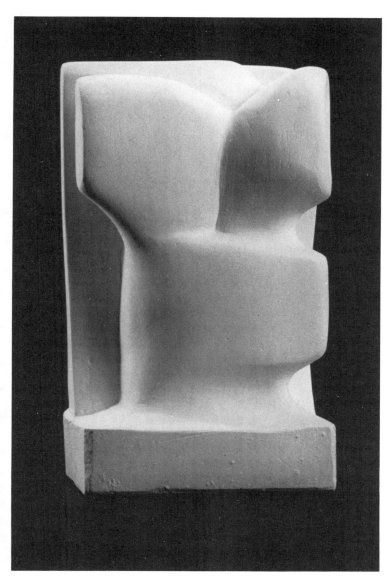

Fig. 6–11. Highlights and shadows can add dramatic impact. [Stephen Issler (student). (Photo by Unhjem/Cavallo).]

metal file first. The curved end will allow you to file across both convex and concave forms. All contours of a good metal file are abrasive, not merely the flat ends, so use the tips and edges for hard to reach areas.

Understand that you are not *smoothing* but continuing to *model* the forms that have been carved with the knife or

Fig. 6–12. To remove imperfections such as indentations and hollows, you might file the form (as indicated by the dotted line). This will reduce it in size but retain the essential form.

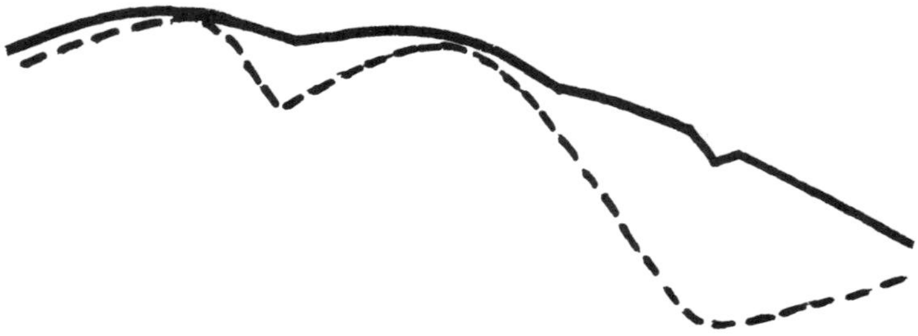

Fig. 6–13. "Imperfections" can also help you to imagine further cuts that may be more effective, and stimulate you to carve even more deeply (as indicated by dotted line).

the mallet and chisel. You may be concerned that the forms will be unnecessarily scratched with the file if you want the final surface to be smooth. But remember that a smooth surface laid over a rough roadbed results in just that: a rough road with a smooth coat. You want clear, solid, definite forms, all *chosen* by you, not simply *settled for.* You do not want waves and bumps unless waves and bumps are an integral part of your sculpture; you do not want interference with form, only the form itself (see figures 6–1 and 6–14). When you use the file, think of form, not surface. A final surface smoothness, if desired, will be accomplished with the wet/dry papers.

After filing, you are ready to use the black Carborundum papers. Use the coarse grit first and proceed to progressively finer grits as scratches are removed. Wet the paper as you sand; the water keeps the paper from becoming coated with sediment. Tear the paper into manageable-size pieces as you work, bending and folding them as needed to reach all the surfaces. The plaster smoothes easily because it is soft; therefore, if you are having difficulty, it is probably because you are using too fine a paper at that particular stage.

When the sculpture is finished and dry, it is advisable to

Fig. 6–14. An example of a well-finished plaster carving with no abrasions to interfere with the flow of forms. [John Reda (student). (Photo by Lee Vold).]

spray it to protect against fingerprints and dust. Use a clear plastic such as Flecto Varethane, which comes in either a gloss or satin finish.

Filing the Cement and Vermiculite Carving

For finishing the cement and vermiculite carving, you will need a flat chisel and a file that is moderately coarse. Sanding is not recommended, since a very smooth texture tends to obliterate the vitality provided by the vermiculite particles and can give the finished piece the appearance of dull and dusty cement. That does not mean the forms should not be fully developed in terms of shape. Figure 6–1 is an example of clearly defined forms obtained by careful filing of the broad shapes created by mallet and chisel. Modeling forms in the cement and vermiculite block is often best done with files to deepen, round, and more fully develop them.

If negative forms—holes and open spaces—have been carved into the block, be sure, when finishing, to file the inner as well as the outer contours (figure 6–15).

Fig. 6–15. In finishing, the inner as well as the outer shapes must be critically viewed and contoured. [Michele Nolin (student). Cement and vermiculite. (Photo by Lee Vold).]

The Final Decisions

Whether you work predominately with the chisel or with the knife, whether you deliberately leave rough cuts in the finished piece or tailor your forms with the file, how much you use the distinctive characteristics of the poured block and how much of it you change—these are largely a matter of style. What is important is that your decisions be based on what you are *striving for,* and not what you have *settled for.* Ask yourself this question as you reach the final stages of carving and slowly turn your sculpture to critically regard each view of it: "Is this something I have selected or something I have settled for?"

Mounting

Your final decisions in carving, as in every project, will involve mounting your finished piece (or pieces if you have made two forms in relationship). Both the plaster and the cement and vermiculite sculptures can be drilled with masonry bits and mounted according to the guidelines given in chapter 9. Both materials are soft and not at all brittle; therefore, there is little danger of your sculptures shattering when drilled. A list of necessary materials needed for mounting, together with suggestions for how your piece might be positioned, are included in chapter 9.

EXTENDING THE PROJECT: ART IN HUMAN SERVICE

Plaster is easy to find, transport, prepare, and clean up and is therefore a good sculptural medium to use in situations not particularly designed for art workshops. The projects suggested can be imaginatively modified to suit the special interests of participants.

Shapes

The object of this project is to pour plaster to make shapes; to see something in the shapes; and to then refine the shapes by filing, sanding, or painting.

Materials: waxed paper; plaster; three-ounce paper or plastic cups; coffee stirrers; nail; sandpaper (medium grit); watercolors and brush (optional); shellac and alcohol (optional); wooden base (optional); plastic bowl (three-quart size or smaller, depending on the number of participants); Five Minute Epoxy resin (or white glue if resin presents a problem).

Procedure: Spread sheets of waxed paper on a smooth table surface, one for each participant. Mix plaster in a plastic bowl according to instructions on page 98. After stirring, pour quickly into paper cups. Each participant is given a cup containing the liquid plaster.

The cup is squeezed slightly to form a spout, after which shapes are poured onto the waxed paper. Avoid very thin "tails," as these will break off. Use the coffee stirrers to push the plaster around if desired. Do not manipulate after the plaster begins to set (approximately five minutes). When hard (approximately twenty minutes), select those plaster shapes that you like and refine them with sandpaper if they need work. Paint the shapes if further definition is wanted. Shellac and alcohol mixed in equal parts makes a slightly glossy off-white finish. The shapes can be glued onto a piece of wood and prepared with wire and screw eyes for hanging.

Jewelry

Materials: see "Shapes." Add pin backs and leather cord (both optional).

Procedure: follow the procedure for "Shapes." When the plaster shape is almost set, make a nail hole. After finishing, string a leather cord through the hole to serve as a chain. Alternatively, a pin back can be glued to the back of the shape.

Carving Cups

Materials: see "Shapes." Add a paring knife.

Procedure: Pour the plaster into cups and let it harden. When it has set (about twenty minutes) and you are ready to carve, peel the cup back and carve the block with a paring knife.

When you prepare the project for "Shapes," have cups on hand ready to fill in case there is leftover plaster. For variation, fill only the bottom of the cups to form round shapes; then combine these to make relief compositions or bore a nail hole and incise them decoratively with any pointed instrument to make hanging pendants.

Making the Head in Clay 7

THE project presented in this chapter is the least improvisational, most structured in the text. You will need some patience to follow through with it and will probably be spending more concentrated time on it than you have on the other projects. In addition to trying to model the structure and features of the head, you are asked to do a great deal of new "looking" to build a consciousness of the sculptural elements that comprise this most fascinating subject.

If you work the recommended ten hours per week, you will be devoting forty hours to the project. (Your actual working time, as in other projects, is a variable that can only be set by you.) If you do not complete the project in that time, do not be dismayed, for the head is a complex, highly elusive anatomical entity, and many contacts with your medium and models are needed to develop a true understanding of it.

THE VALUE AND OBJECTIVES OF THE PROJECT

The head, in addition to its biological role as the center for sensory stimulation, thought processes, and emotional functioning, is also an aesthetic organization of forms. The human head is a physical entity worthy of study by the sculptor, quite apart from the harmony and hues of facial features that so intrigue the portrait painter but are conveyed in nonchromatic sculpture only by light and shadow.

Looking at the sculpture in figure 7–1, *Oriel Ross* by Jacob Epstein, one is impressed with the dramatic use of planes and the full development of shapes in the arrangement of facial features at the hand of the sculptor: the broad planes of the cheek descending to the sharp boundary of the jaw; the circularity of the eye sockets against the angular ridges of forehead and nose; the projecting planes in the structure of the mouth against the lyrical curves of the lips; and so on.

Fig. 7–1. Observe the clearly defined features. Notice the structure of the planes in the cheeks, nose, and mouth, and the strong modeling of the hollows and highlights. [Jacob Epstein, *Oriel Ross* (1932); Bronze, 26¾″ × 17″. Collection, The Museum of Modern Art, New York. Gift of Edward M. M. Warburg.]

Of course, the head is never viewed purely as an arrangement of forms. Body and soul, personality and mood, achievement and despair are all reflected in the facial features. Your observations and your speculations about the human behind the head will become a very natural part of your efforts to create the head in clay. Moreover, through your explorations in this provocative study, you may come closer to an intimate understanding of the spirit and substance of sculpture.

APPROACH

Read through the points below before you begin, to gain an overall perspective on what you will be doing and to help you prepare.

The Model

You will need a model who will be able to sit for you during the times you can work. If no model is available, it is a better learning experience to use your own reflection in the mirror, rather than a photograph. Doing so will allow you to touch the three-dimensional forms as you see them and thereby increase your understanding of them. An exception to the use of photographs is Margit Malmstrom's photographic record of Bruno Lucchesi modeling the head from start to finish, a book that is a good visual supplement to this chapter (see *References*).

In this first experience of modeling the head, there should be no overt attempt to achieve a likeness of your model. Rather, you should try to concentrate on the structural elements of the head and its features. There may also be times when you want to continue working after the model has left. In that case, since you are not striving for a likeness, you can use some of your own features as a reference. The ear, for example, is a complex pattern of forms that requires a great deal of close inspection and many modeling attempts before it is understood, and those attempts are often effectively done by examining your own reflection as you work.

When working with a model, seat him or her at eye level at a distance that enables you to see the whole head at once. Your own position should be standing, facing both your work and the model, with your work at eye level on a surface that turns easily. The lighting in the room should be excellent.

Size

The head in clay need not be life-size for you to have a successful experience. In this exercise, it is expected that the head will be approximately one-half to three-quarter life-size and modeled with kiln or oven-firing clay—the choice will depend on whether or not a kiln is available to you—with no armature used for support. If you wish to make a larger head or a "bust" that includes shoulders, an armature will be required for support. (See *References* under "Clay-Methods"; Padovano, *The Process of Sculpture* for information on constructing armatures for larger works destined for casting; and refer to Lucchesi and Malmstrom, *Terra Cotta: The Technique of Fired Clay Sculpture* for making armatures for larger works destined for firing.)

Preparing for Kiln Firing

If at all feasible, try to make prearrangements for firing the finished sculpture. If there is a facility that will do this for you, you may be asked to use their clay so that your piece will be compatible with others to be loaded in the kiln at the same time. It is wise to actively pursue the search for a kiln, as the detailed modeling and texture problems that apply to modeling the head make laminating (described in chapter 2 as an alternative to firing) unsuitable.

CHECKLIST OF TOOLS AND MATERIALS

The tools listed in chapter 2, "Modeling in Clay," illustrated in figures 2–2 and 2–3, are the same as those that will be needed for this project.

METHOD

The method given in this section has been developed by the author specifically for beginners. There are other methods of forming the head and features that you may find equally good. And certainly there are more in-depth, detailed, and anatomically oriented books that you may want to study, should you develop an interest in portrait sculpture.

Because this exercise is likely to be a first experience in modeling the head, the reader is cautioned not to strive for "perfection." That is, one's aim should not be, for example, to render the satin surface of baby-smooth skin; attention to surface detail in these early attempts to produce the head tends to impede concentration on structure and form and moreover often results in "slick" rather than smooth textures. To reinforce the focus on structure and form, no attempt was made in the terra cotta head modeled by the author—views of which are illustrated below—to be fastidious about surface detail. In this regard, the grog, besides giving the sculpture strength and greater flexibility to withstand firing, may help you to ignore suface fussiness in this first venture into the realm of portraiture, though admittedly, the grog particles can occasionally be frustrating.

Clay Preparation

Because you may want to fire the clay head when it is finished, the clay should be prepared and applied carefully to eliminate air bubbles that may later cause the piece to break in the kiln or oven. To prepare the clay, throw three large mounds of clay several times onto a clean, firm surface. Keep the mounds tightly covered with plastic when they are not being used. Get in the habit of collecting clay fragments as they fall and pressing them into the mound; the smaller the size, the faster clay will dry and your object is to keep your clay the same consistency throughout.

Pointers Regarding Clay Application

As you add clay, make sure you press it firmly and evenly onto the form. Merely daubing the clay in place will allow air to fill the openings; the added pieces will then dry more quickly than the rest of the form and probably fall off. Clay may be pressed on with the thumbs and modeled, or slabs of clay may be fitted and pressed on to contour a desired form. It may be useful at this time to reread the sections "Clay Preparation" and "Repairs" in chapter 2, including the technique of bonding clay parts by scoring and adding slip.

Various parts of the head suggest certain shapes. Therefore, it is often helpful to make the shape—such as a flat slab or a coil—in your hands and then press that onto the main form. This is a particularly useful technique when working on the high ridges of the ear and on the distinctive masses comprising the hair.

FORMING THE STRUCTURE OF THE HEAD

Begin by repeatedly throwing two of the large wedged mounds together to form a rectangular block. This will be the basic mass of the head; therefore, if it is smaller than you want your head to be, throw a third mound into it until you have a mound of comfortable size to begin with—one large enough to allow you to see clearly what you are doing. The head will get larger as you work, but the starting mass will be your approximate scale. Two-thirds of this mass will become the head, and the remaining one-third will be used for the neck. Lightly draw a line with your wooden tool to indicate this division.

With the rectangle held upright, designate what is to be the front of the head by drawing a vertical line along the center. The purpose of this line is only to differentiate the front from the back and sides as you begin to build up the forms; it will soon be erased. Using both a small wooden block and your hands, begin the dual processes of carving and shaping to change the rectangular shape to an oval. Use the block to push the clay upwards as much as possible rather than downwards, to compensate for the fact that moist clay tends to sag as it is worked.

The head is essentially an oval shape that sits on a cylindrical neck (figure 7–2). Note that the high point of the head is at the crown (figure 7–3), and the direction of the neck has a forward pitch.

Block in the ears and the jaw as these relate to the neck and the base of the skull, observing that the base of the ear is the juncture of the jaw, the neck, and the base of the skull (figure 7–4). Do not attempt to form the ears, merely block in their placement in relation to the jaw, neck, and skull. Consideration of the shape of the ear and its placement in relation to the profile lines of brow and nose will be given later. Use the wooden blocks as supports under the chin if the clay begins to sag. Refer to the pointers regarding clay application given earlier in this chapter as you work.

BLOCKING IN THE FEATURES

When the head and neck have been formed and are properly shaped when seen from all sides, you are ready to begin the features. If the features are formed before the shape of the head is adequately made, you will probably spend much unnecessary time reforming them because they are in the wrong location.

The Basic "T" Shape

Erase the original vertical line designating the front of the head (if it is not already gone by this time). Using the edge of your tool, draw a curved eye line across the front of the head. Now draw a "T," using the eyeline as the top horizontal bar (figure 7–5). From the vertical trunk of the "T" will emerge the nose, mouth, and chin.

Divide the vertical trunk of the "T" with three horizontal lines, as shown in figure 7–6.

With the serrated edge of your wooden tool or with the blade—whichever seems most comfortable—carve a curved diagonal plane on each side of the face, from the outer corner of the designated eye area to the base of the nose, to form the high ridges of the cheek bones. Carve away from the midline of the lips upward and inward to the base of the nose. Carve away from the midline of the lips downward and inward to the beginning of the chin (figure 7–7).

The Interior and Exterior Profile Lines

Turning the head to the side, curve the vertical "T" line to form the *interior profile line,* as shown in figure 7–8. The interior profile line begins at the outermost corner of the eye socket and ends at the jowl. Following the contour of the exterior profile, note that it touches the interior profile line subtly, at the nostril and at the midline of the lips.

Seen frontally, the eyes, nose, mouth, and chin all curve symmetrically from their highest point at the center around to each side to meet the interior profile line at the outer corners of the eyes, the nostrils, the lips, and the chin. Observing this will help you to prevent the features from growing away from the head. Extending the features too far outward as they are being modeled is a common pitfall that occurs in early attempts to sculpt the head. The features, being more interesting and more visually obvious than the structure of the skull, get such close attention that they often tend to be worked as entities of their own. If you refer periodically to the interior profile line as you continue to work, you may avoid that situation. Note that this contour is as significant a distinguishing characteristic of your model as is the *exterior profile line.*

It should be stressed that the interior profile line may be

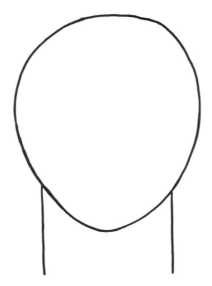

Fig. 7–2. For this project, think of the head as an oval shape that sits on a cylindrical neck.

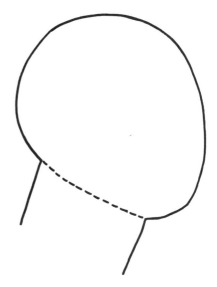

Fig. 7–3. The direction of the neck has a forward pitch; the crown of the head is the highest point.

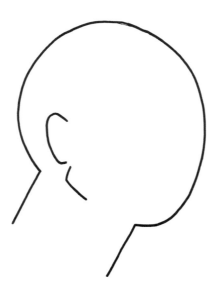

Fig. 7–4. The back of the ear at its base is the juncture point where the jaw, the top of the neck, and the base of the skull meet.

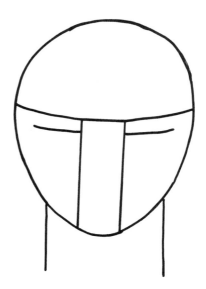

Fig. 7–5. The basic "T" shape: the horizontal lines designate the area of the eyes. From the vertical trunk of the "T" will emerge the nose, mouth, and chin.

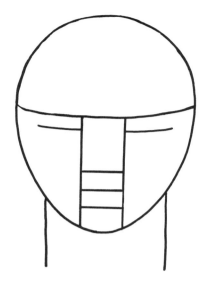

Fig. 7–6. The "T" is divided with three horizontal lines.

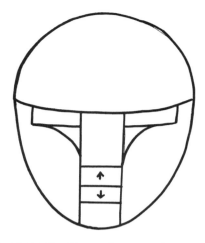

Fig. 7–7. The diagonal curves designate the high ridges of the cheeks. Carve away from the midline of the lips and inward to the base of the nose and downward and inward to the beginning of the chin.

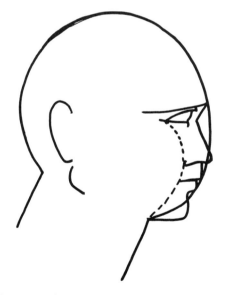

Fig. 7–8. The *interior profile line* is indicated by a dotted line. It begins at the outermost corner of the eye socket and ends as the jowl, appearing and disappearing at various points according to your model. The *exterior profile line* returns to meet this line at the outer edges of the nostrils and lips.

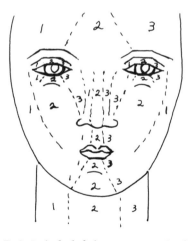

Fig. 7–9. It is helpful to view each of the features of the face as an organization of three planes: a top plane (2) and two side planes (1 and 3).

121

quite obvious at one point and may disappear entirely at another. It might be seen clearly in profile only at the corners of the nostrils and the lips and more clearly in the three-quarter views when it becomes an outer contour. In any case, it is a subtle line. Unduly emphasized, the line will age your portrait of the model and, interestingly enough, may also reveal how the model will look in years to come.

FORMING THE FEATURES

A good way to begin to observe the individual features of the face is to view each of them as an organization of three planes: a top plane and two side planes, seen in figure 7–9 as horizontal and diagonal lines, respectively.

Use the flat blade of your modeling tool to define these planes as they are described in this section. Be aware that there are no sharp lines of delineation between planes; rather, one plane meets another to form a subtle high point or ridge. The contours that are formed as planes meet will be infinitely variable from portrait to portrait and may even vary, to some extent, between the two sides of a single face.

As the features in this section are described, it is suggested that you examine the various views of the head illustrated in figures 7–10 to 7–15.

The Nose

Begin the nose by carving the V-shaped depression at the base of the brow. Add clay to the length and bridge of the nose according to the general shape seen in your model. Viewing only the shaft of the nose and not the nostrils, try to see the three planes—a top and two sides. From the side view try to observe the three planes of the nostril, though from this viewpoint, they are likely to merge into a sweeping curve.

The deep cavities of the nostrils are important to indicate, as these are orifices that lead into the body. As with the mouth, revealing the dark shadows of their depth can help give life to your portrait. Use the blade of your wooden tool to carve into the nostrils while shaping the exterior curves with your fingers. Use your wooden blade and your fingers to define the flat underside of each nostril and the rounded contour at the tip of the nose.

Fig. 7–10. Note the inner profile line, which curves gently from the *outer corners* of the eye, the nostrils, and the lips, disappearing in the jowl. Note also the forward pitch of the neck. Carried upwards, it is in line with the pitch of the underside of the brow as it meets the nose. The planes of the mouth jut outward from the base of the nose and from the crevice of the chin. (Photo by Lee Vold).

The Mouth

Students sometimes begin by thinking of the mouth as simply two lips—a top and a bottom, with an opening in between. This concept may originate from the customary adolescent drawing of the mouth as a set of cute bow lips. Actually, each lip might better be thought of as an edging of the mouth, similar in concept to the lip that forms a table's edge.

The mouth itself is a structure that takes its shape from what supports it underneath, namely the teeth. The upper teeth project outward and downward from the base of the nose and so does the upper portion of the mouth that covers them; the lower teeth project outward and upward from the base of the chin and so does the lower portion of the mouth that covers them.

Three planes are visible in both the upper and lower portions of the mouth—a top plane and two side planes in each section. Form these planes in the upper section, projecting them outward and downward from the base of the nose. Now make a depression in the center of the top plane. The high points created on either side of this division will form the high points of the top lip. Form the three planes of the lower section of the mouth, projecting them outward and upward from the base of the chin.

You are now ready to form the lips. The high points of the top and bottom lips may be difficult to see clearly, but they form a sensuous and perfect fit as they meet at the midline. Notice that after each high point or swelling, there is a dip or depression. These forms may be subtle or pronounced depending, of course, on your model, but if you try to see them as planes—and the swellings and dips created as these planes meet—the mouth may not be as confusing to render as it seems.

The lips enclose the orifice of the mouth, and the deep shadow of their partition is rendered as the lip itself is modeled and defined: press the edge of the thin-bladed plastic tool between the lips; then, while accentuating the rich curves and fullness of the lips as you follow their contours, pull the lip outward against your fingertips, thereby making an edge—or, literally, a lip. Observe the swellings and depressions of the lips when seen from both the front and the side views. Go close to your model to observe this; use mirrors to study

Fig. 7–11. The center plane of the mouth is divided by a groove, the high ridges of the groove define the corresponding high points of the lips. The pupils in this modeling of the head are deeply carved to indicate dark, penetrating eyes. [Judith Peck, sculptor. (Photo by Lee Vold).]

your own reflection; and examine this feature in figures 7–10 to 7–13.

The Chin

The chin also has three planes, but the transition between the top plane and those on either side is quite gentle. In profile, the chin does not project as far forward as the nose. Keep this guideline in mind as you work, to avoid building the jaw and chin out too far.

The Forehead

Like the other features, there are many variations of the forehead, but again, it is helpful to see the forehead as an organization of three planes—a surface and two sides. The subtle divisions between planes, if they are evident at all, may appear as diagonal or near-vertical shadows and will usually be more prominent on males than on females. The forehead might also be viewed as a broader version of the chin—a sweeping curve from side to side.

When you study your model in profile, note carefully the relationship between forehead and chin in terms of:

- the extent of their forward projections: for example, does the chin project further out than the forehead? How much?
- their directions: is the slant of the chin about the same as the forehead or is it different? How is it different?
- their sizes: how much smaller is the form of the chin than the forehead?

Posing questions about the relationship of one feature to another forces you to see aspects of line, shape, mass, movement, and proportion that you might not have been aware of in studying a single feature in isolation. Try to make those comparisons while looking at figure 7–10.

The Eyes and Eye Sockets

The eyes are formed in this study by first creating sockets into which they will be placed. The eye is well protected by bone structure on *all four sides:* the forehead on the top and outer sides; the bony structure of the nose on the inner side; and the cheekbone below. Create the eye sockets by carving within these perimeters.

Fig. 7–12. A rim is carved to indicate a division of coloring in the iris, more common in blue and green eyes than in brown. (Photo by Lee Vold).

Fig. 7–13. Clay remains in the eye cavities to catch the light and project a less stark, more thoughtful look. (Photo by Lee Vold).

The eye is a circular form, a ball. Only a small portion of the eye is visible; the rest is set deeply into the head. The placement of the eyeball in the head follows the slant of the brow and the cheekbone—those bony structures that protect it. That is, the eyeball is set into the skull on a diagonal, not straight up and down. Failure to recognize this may lead you to model eyes that appear to be falling out. A good way to begin constructing the eye is to make a ball the right size for the socket and press it firmly into the socket on its diagonal tilt.

The top eyelid drapes over the upper portion of the eye, following the contour of the eyeball. From the side, that lid will therefore project outward. The bottom lid, smaller in size, drapes over the bottom portion of the eye and also follows the contour of the eyeball. From the side, therefore, it too projects outward. Note that the upper lid projects further forward than the lower lid when seen from the side, following the diagonal slant of the eye socket. Note also that the swelling of the eyeball against the lower lid may continue to have a ripple effect below the eye.

After the lids are in place you will need to reemphasize the ball shape of the eye and create the deep lines that indicate that an orifice is being described. With your small, curved plastic tool, firmly round the outermost contour of each eyeball to set it inside the lids more definitely. The eyeballs are always inside the lids and never extend beyond them; be sure that this is so in your modeling.

Between the upper lid and the eyebrow is an area that has a distinctive shape; its contour influences the line of the upper lid. Observe that area carefully and then model it with your flat-bladed tool to define the planes, the contours, and the shadows it creates.

The hairy portion of the eyebrow, like hair itself (described below), is composed of mass and texture. Therefore, model the forms that you see, being careful to observe the *whole* brow formation, not simply the hair; then texture the strands of hair with your thin plastic tool in the direction in which they seem to grow.

The *iris* is the circular colored portion of the eye; in the center of this is the opening or *pupil*. The surrounding white portion is the *sclera*. The eyeball is frequently left smooth and unbroken, but some sculptors prefer to indicate the iris and pupil to focus the eyes and make the head come alive; and also to indicate through degrees of light and shadow, the

Fig. 7–14. Hair is essentially mass and texture. Look first for the configuration of the large hair masses; then look for the direction of the strands within the masses; in accentuating those directions, you are modeling texture and "hair style." (Photo by Lee Vold).

color of the eyes. To do this effectively and symmetrically may require several attempts; a matched set is not so easy to make; trial and error is probably the best way. Simple circular holes will not do, as there should be some clay to catch the light so that the eyes do not appear hollow and lifeless. The deeper the penetration, the darker the shadow and the darker the eye will appear. Blue eyes would be indicated with a lighter, more delicate carving of the iris. Three different treatments of the eyes are illustrated in figures 7–11, 7–12, and 7–13 and described in the captions.

The Ears

A guideline to use in placing the ear is that the top of the ear is usually in line with the top of the brow, and the bottom of the ear is in line with the base of the nose.

Seen from the rear, the base of the ear is a critical landmark, as it is there that one can see the merger of the jaw, the neck, and the base of the skull. The size and placement of the two ears should be checked from both rear view and front view.

Seen from the side, the outer shape of the ear is roughly an oval. The inner shape of the ear is roughly an S-curve. The ear is an orifice; therefore, its cavity should be defined along with the less prominent but equally distinctive depressions and ridges that comprise this seemingly complicated form. Try to model the shapes that you see sharply and crisply, carving the planes and curves with the wooden tool and using the wire tool for detail. Observe the high ridges and depressions and try to determine, in both the side and the front views, what is outermost (a high point), what is next outermost, etc. Try to contour the ear as much as possible by identifying planes and projections rather than seeing only a maze of shapes. Your own reflection may help you to see this feature more clearly. Use a double mirror, as the clue to successful execution is repeated observations from all three views.

HAIR

Hair often looks to beginning sculptors to be a grand tangle (literally) that they will never understand. The problem may become a more manageable one if you think of hair as essentially two things: mass and texture.

The mass constitutes the various shapes and layers that

are seen in the hair style. You can attack these masses by pressing clay slabs and coils onto the form in the general configuration that the mass seems to have. The heel of your hand, your fingers, the wooden block, and the flat-bladed wooden tool will all be called into service at this stage.

Texture indicates the pattern and direction that the strands of hair take within the mass. You might want to use other implements, such as a thick, stiff scrub brush or a comb, to help you achieve these patterns.

Light and shadow are essential characteristics of hair. Dark hair can be conveyed by accentuating shadows. Note that varying shadows appear between the strands, and that they are especially dark in places where hair is bound and where it falls against the face, the neck, and the collar. Refer to figure 7–1 to observe Jacob Epstein's handling of the mass and direction of hair strands in his portrait of Oriel Ross.

HOLLOWING AND DRYING

Reread the sections in chapter 2 on "Repairs" and "Drying: Hollowing and Storage," with reference to completing the head. The head may be larger than your previous clay sculptures and, moreover, more time may have been invested in it. You will therefore want to approach the hollowing process with care and with the following points in mind. Be sure that:

- the sculpture is firm (but not dry);
- you separate it completely and carefully from its base (with a piece of wire);
- that an adequate quantity of soft rags has been placed under it when you lay it down upon its back to hollow it.

If the head is not too large or cumbersome, you can leave it in one piece and scoop out the clay from the bottom, as described in chapter 2. If, however, the head seems too large, too cumbersome, or too delicate to risk laying down, use this alternative method of hollowing:

1. Separate the head into two parts with a piece of wire, slicing it from top to bottom just behind the ears (figure 7–16). Remove only the back half, leaving the front to remain securely on the base (figure 7–17).

Fig. 7–15. Try to simplify the features by creating planes wherever possible and concentrating on the inner and outer contours rather than the many facial lines and grooves that will both confuse you and age the portrait of the model. (Photo by Lee Vold).

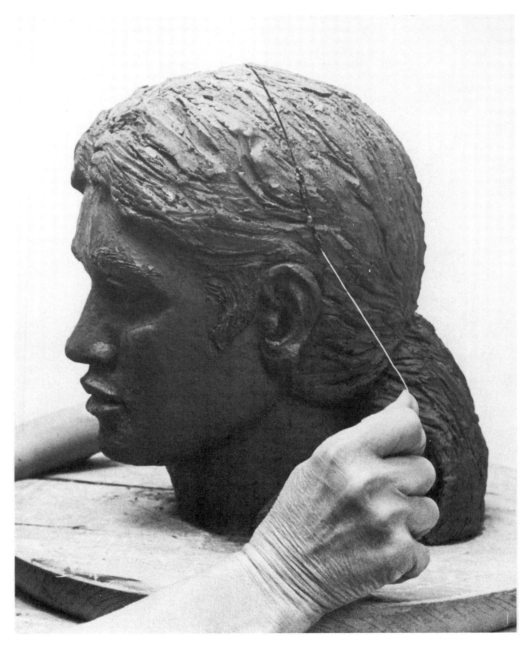

Fig. 7–16. Hollowing: separate the head into two parts, slicing it from top to bottom just behind the ears. (Photo by Lee Vold).

Fig. 7–17. Remove the back half, leaving the front to remain on the base. (Photo by Lee Vold).

2. Hollow the two halves by scooping out clay with the wire end of your tool (figure 7–18), but leave the joining edges intact with a full 1-inch margin (figure 7–19). As you go deeper toward the front of the head, support the chin with a lump of clay to keep it from falling forward.

3. After hollowing, score both halves of the joining edges with crosshatching; then lightly apply slip to the total joining area (figure 7–19).

4. Line up the two halves of the head carefully and press them firmly together (figure 7–20). A support under the chin may be necessary to keep the head upright; if your head seems vulnerable to tipping, support it with clay where needed throughout the hollowing procedure.

5. Pinch the edges all around the seam and add more clay as needed. Repair the area by modeling and texturing again.

The head will be considerably more vulnerable to damage after hollowing. Therefore, make sure that it is securely attached to the working base. Secure it with extra clay, if needed, before you attempt further work on it. Then, work with care on repairs and on the finishing touches.

Whichever method of hollowing you use, it is a good idea to make one or two pin holes with a very thin nail in the top of the head to allow steam to escape. Finally, dry and store the head according to the procedures given in chapter 2.

EXTENDING THE PROJECT: ART IN HUMAN SERVICE

The head is a popular subject for creative three-dimensional endeavors. Human heads and not-so-human heads, from monsters to Martians, are subject matter for the project. The stance, the features, and the expression given to clay sculptures of the head project human emotions and can be a good starting point for individual or group discussions.

Formal guidelines for modeling the head in clay need not be observed, as participants may not have sufficient patience or interest to follow through with the procedures; moreover, the logistics of scheduling might limit the opportunity to

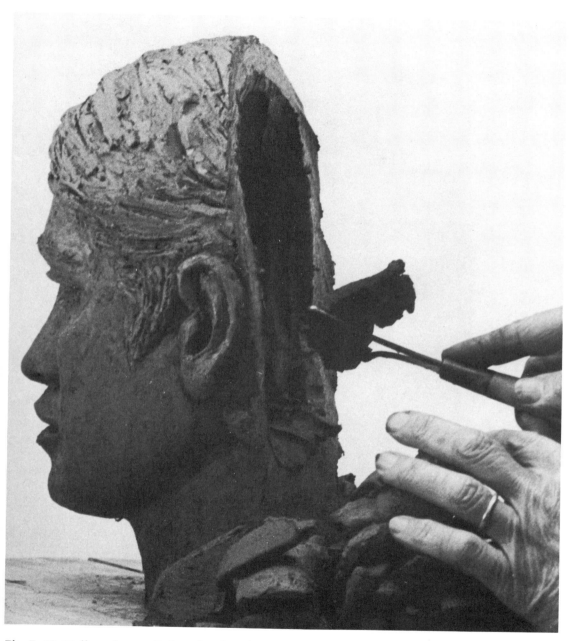

Fig. 7–18. Hollow the two halves, leaving the joining edges intact with a one-inch margin. Remember to try for a one-inch thickness of clay throughout. (Photo by Lee Vold).

Fig. 7–19. After hollowing, crosshatch the joining edges and lightly add slip. (Photo by Lee Vold).

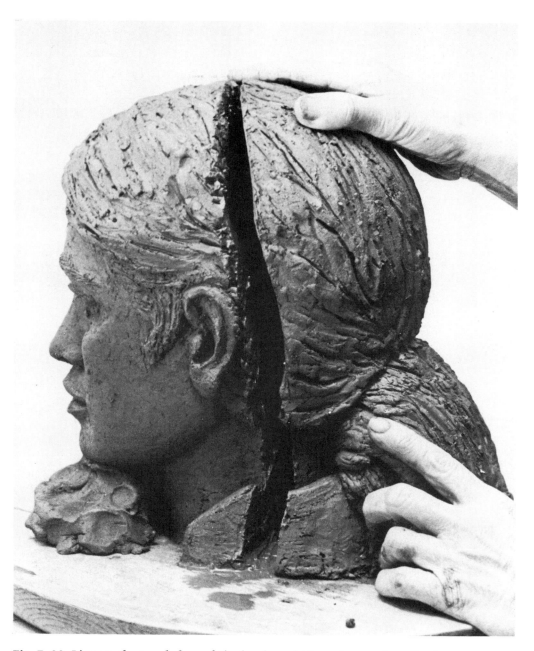

Fig. 7–20. Line up the two halves of the head carefully and press them firmly together; note the support placed under the chin to prevent the head from tipping forward. (Photo by Lee Vold).

pursue technique in depth. If, however, there is interest, time, and opportunity, instructions—including the "T" and the initial carving of the facial planes—can be reasonably offered.

Whether or not any of the guidelines included in this chapter are utilized, participants should be encouraged in the *personal content* aspect of the project. This might be accomplished in a number of ways, for example:

- giving a personality to the sculpture;
- finding resemblances to one's self or other people in one or more of the facial features;
- discussing the attitudes, emotions, or thoughts of the "person" in the sculpture.

The project, in any case, should be a vehicle for having a good time through the opportunity of creating this most interesting physical aspect of people—their faces.

Working in Wax

2 WEEKS

Wax, when heated to the right consistency, can be manipulated and modeled. In this respect it has properties that are similar to clay, and many artists create sculptures in wax that are intended for future casting in bronze, just as they do with clay. Clay, however, must remain soft in order to be manipulated, and its constant flexibility can work to the sculptor's disadvantage because of the need to support the clay as it is built up. That support may require the construction of an armature before any forms are modeled. Armatures limit the freedom to change forms while the work is underway.

Wax sculptures require support as well, but wax is essentially flexible only with the application of heat. No armature or external support system is needed, because wax in the form of rods can be welded in place to provide support for work in progress. The position and curvature of the rods can be changed if the design changes. Various types of wax have varying degrees of hardness and softness, allowing some to be used specifically for support and others for modeling and texturing.

The disadvantage of wax as a sculptural medium is its impermanence. The heat needed to manipulate wax is the same heat, unfortunately, that is found in radiators and hot sun. Therefore, unless the sculptures are kept reasonably cool, they will eventually collapse, the harder forms of wax lasting the longest.

The traditional method of preserving wax sculptures is casting them in bronze, a technical process usually done in a foundry. Wax sculptures can also be cast in other metals and in materials such as plaster, plastics (clear resins or resins bonded to bronze or stone powders), concrete, and so on. (See *References* for resources on casting.)

Another method for preserving wax, and one that can be used in the home studio, is lamination of the forms with a more permanent covering. The materials and procedures for

Fig. 8–1. Texture compliments form. Here, flat textures enhance the lyrical circularity of line and form. [Judith Peck, *Park Avenue Pup*; bronze; approximately 16″ high, 3″ × 3″ at base. Collection, Louis Lefkowitz. Wax for bronze casting. (Photo by Jules Pinsley).]

applying surface lamination are described later in this chapter.

Wax can be purchased in block or sheet form, or sheets can be made by melting the block in the home oven (described below). The sheets can be cut and welded to form flat constructions, very different stylistically from wax modeling. Because basic principles of welding are used in such construction—albeit on a much less complicated scale—wax welding might serve as a good preliminary exercise for future welding in metal. The procedures for preparing, cutting, welding, forming, modeling, texturing, and finishing wax are described in this chapter.

THE BASIC MEDIUM

The terminology below is offered to assist you when ordering various waxes from a supplier. To begin an initial project requiring little support, however, you may need only a slab of microcrystalline wax, obtainable from sculpture supply houses.

- Microcrystalline wax slabs (brown): thick 2-inch slabs for breaking into pieces and softening; used for modeling and for preparing wax sheets;
- Microcrystalline wax sheets of $\frac{1}{8}$-inch thickness (black or brown); used for cutting into patterns to create forms;
- Square cored $\frac{1}{2}$-inch × $\frac{1}{2}$-inch hollow wax rods—sprues (factory colored red): used to provide solid support for long vertical designs;
- Round solid $\frac{1}{4}$-inch wax rods—sprues (factory colored green): thinner rods, used to connect and support angular forms.

Note: colors may vary with manufacturer.

CHECKLIST OF TOOLS AND MATERIALS

A significant advantage to fabricating sculptures in wax is the relative simplicity of the tools and materials needed to do the job. The items listed below (and shown in figure 8–2) are suitable for all aspects of sculptural fabrication in wax: supporting the forms, cutting, welding, modeling, applying wax, and texturing. Some items are recommended

Fig. 8–2. Tools and materials for wax forming. (Photo by Lee Vold).

but listed as optional: the thermostatically controlled wax melter can reduce frustration and increase efficiency, but it is not a requisite; because it is expensive, other ways of softening wax are offered in the text. In the interests of further economy, an alcohol burner or even a candle can substitute for the soldering iron; however, these items are considerably less efficient. The various products suggested for lamination are not listed here.

- Soldering iron (electric hot knife): to heat tools, soften wax, and join wax sheets and rods.
- Wax tool with small flat oval blade: to apply wax and model forms.
- Paring knife (thin-bladed): heated and used for cutting operations.
- Putty knife (not shown): for clean-up operations.
- Lazy Susan; placed under work board for easy turning.
- Wooden base: to use as work board.
- Nail brush or small scrub brush and green soap for washing hands (not shown).

- Protective covering for floor and table as needed. (Newspapers are adequate for the floor; an old Formica table is suggested as a work surface.)
- Alcohol burner and denatured alcohol: can be used as substitute for soldering iron.
- Candle: can be used as substitute for soldering iron.
- Electric wax melter (optional)—a thermostatically controlled heater: to melt wax to consistencies desired for various applications.
- Thin cotton cloth: for rubbing smooth textures (optional).
- Thin cotton material: for drapery (optional—not shown).
- Cookie tin or pan: for pouring wax sheets (not shown).
- Waxed paper: for pouring wax sheets (not shown).

PREPARATION

Preparation essentially involves (1) having the kind of wax and materials on hand that will permit you to execute your sculpture and (2) having an appropriate and safe place in which to work. Not all of the materials and preparation described may be needed for the sculpture you create, as there is much variety in the design of wax forms. For example, low forms may not require any wax rods for support; small modeled forms may not require wax sheets, only fragments broken from the block. In this initial effort, it is suggested that you begin with an uncomplicated form, one that requires a minimum of support and welding.

Pouring Wax Sheets

Sheets of wax are useful for creating broad forms. These sheets can be purchased through wax or sculpture supply houses or made in the home studio following this procedure:

1. Melt the brown microcrystalline wax in the electric melting pot or in a moderately low oven in a pot that you do not plan to use for anything else.
2. Place a sheet of waxed paper on a cookie tin and place the tin on a flat surface.
3. Pour the melted wax onto the sheet to a thickness of approximately $\frac{1}{8}$-inch. Allow to cool.

4. Place another sheet of waxed paper over the hardened wax and repeat the process for each additional sheet that you need. How much wax to melt will depend on the size of your cookie tin and the number of slabs you intend to make. If a slab is shy, melt and add more wax; it will adhere easily. The waxed paper allows the sheets to be separated when ready for use. The pouring wax can be reheated if it begins to solidify.

Setting Up

Your working space should be in an area with good ventilation so that the wax vapor, which forms as the wax melts, can escape. A table surface that can be used solely for wax, such as an inexpensive folding table with a Formica top, is desirable. Be prepared that wax drippings will accumulate on the base and table surface and possibly on the floor. The drippings can be scraped up with the putty knife, and wax stains are removable with turpentine, but it is safer either to protect those surfaces in advance or to work on surfaces where a small amount of wax debris does not matter.

Use a flat piece of wood, tile, or Plexiglas of appropriate dimensions as a base and place the lazy Susan under it for easy turning once the work is underway. Plug in the soldering iron and the wax melter (if used). A tin can over which a 60-watt light bulb is hung can substitute for the wax melter. Lay out the wax rods and the slab of microcrystalline wax. Pre-cut some small sections from the slab by breaking off pieces with chisel and hammer. Place these in the melter or can. Save all wax fragments, large and small, keeping a box for that purpose; aside from the fact that the wax can be remelted, it is stimulating to have an assortment of wax forms to select from when the work is underway.

PROCEDURES FOR WORKING WITH WAX

The steps described and illustrated in this chapter demonstrate a more complicated form than you may be creating. This is done to enable you to take your sculpture as far as you wish. You should extract from the description only what you need to proceed.

Heating the Tools

Heating the blade of the tool is the necessary first step in all wax cutting and application procedures. Wax, in its cool state, is brittle and hard but it cuts like butter under a well-heated blade. Heat the tool by laying the blade on the soldering iron. Always be careful to place hot items in such a way that the table does not burn and your arm, hand, or fingers will not brush up against them while working.

Support: Cutting, Fusing, and Bending Wax Rods

The amount and kind of support needed will depend on a number of factors, in particular, the size and shape of the work and how it is ultimately to be finished. Will it be laminated or cast? If cast, will a plaster mold be made or will it be cast directly from the wax? How complex will the mold have to be? Will it be conventionally cast (solid investment core) or cast in the ceramic shell process, in which case the piece must be made to withstand many dippings in a "batter" of liquid and granules? Several methods of support are described in this chapter, modifiable at the artist's discretion.

To begin, cut the square cored hollow red sprue rods with the heated knife to the appropriate angle or curve that will support your design. Fuse these to the base and to each other. These wax joinings are literally melted into each other. When welding any joint, make sure that the ends to be joined are matched as closely as possible (no air gaps). A tight fit allows the wax to fuse evenly, ensuring a good bond. Pass the hot blade between the ends to be joined and hold the joint together for several seconds until cool (figure 8–3). Reinforce the joint by passing the heated blade or soldering iron lightly around the circumference and adding soft wax as needed (figure 8–4).

The wax rods can be bent to the shapes desired either before or after they are set in place, depending on their projected complexity and accessibility. Since the wax is brittle, the rods might have to be softened slightly to be pliable. This is done either by dipping them in warm water and then bending them or by passing the soldering iron very lightly over the area as you bend the rod into position (figure 8–5). The rods can be rebent as you go along, should your forms change.

Supports can also be constructed from balsa wood or thin

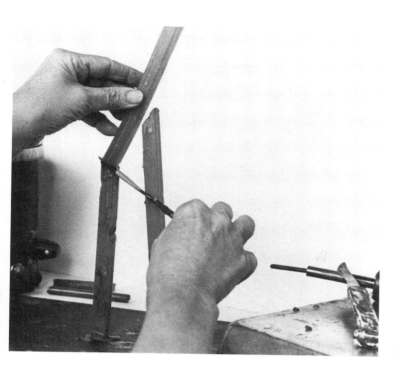

Fig. 8–3. The supporting rods are welded to the base and to each other. A hot blade is passed between the ends to be joined, and the joint is held together for several seconds until cool. Note that to keep the process going, the knife is heating while the tool is in use (and vice versa). (Photo by Lee Vold).

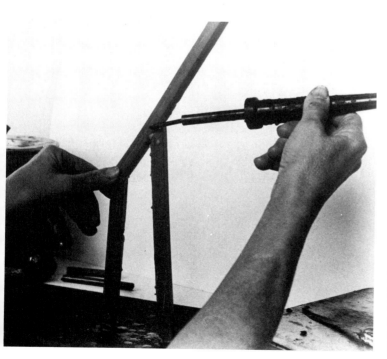

Fig. 8–4. The joint is reinforced by passing the hot blade or soldering iron lightly around the circumference and adding soft wax as needed. (Photo by Lee Vold).

Fig. 8–5. To bend the supporting rod, pass the soldering iron lightly over the area, then slowly bend the rod into position. (Photo by Lee Vold).

Styrofoam sheets, both of which will burn out in a bronze foundry furnace. Wooden toothpicks, which will also burn out, can be used as connectors if needed. The foundry should always be informed about any such materials that are used.

Cutting and Fusing Wax Sheets

The sheet wax is thin and cuts easily with a heated blade. One can be exceedingly free in spirit when cutting out sheet forms for developing into sculptures (figure 8–6). It is a good idea, in order to keep the process going, to heat the blade by resting it on the soldering iron while you use the knife (and vice versa). Because the wax sheets are thinner than the wax rods, they are easy to bend and manipulate with no source of heat other than the warmth of your hands. You can also soften the wax by dipping it in warm water, but dry it after bending and before adding heat to prevent sputtering. Because the sheet wax has little strength of its own, new supports may have to be added as the forms take shape.

Wherever the sheet forms touch one another or the rods, they should be welded fast by delicate fusing. The sheet wax being thinner than the rods requires less heat to melt it

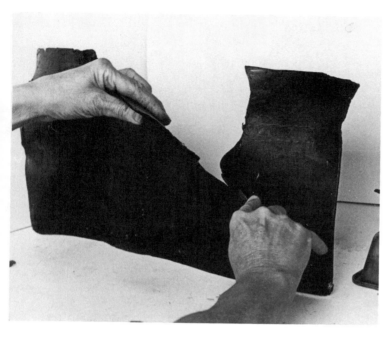

Fig. 8–6. One can be exceedingly free in spirit when cutting out sheet forms for developing into sculpture. (Photo by Lee Vold).

Therefore, lightly melt the edge of the rod first, then touch heat to the sheet and hold (figure 8–7). If holes are melted through the sheet they are easily patched with the addition of more wax. Between sessions the work should be refrigerated to solidify the structure. On removal, remember that whenever soft wax is joined to hardened (cold) wax, the cold surface should be lightly heated to permit good bonding. At this point, the sculpture can change in form and line as your ideas change, inspired by what emerges.

Applying Soft Wax

The electric wax melter allows you to adapt the consistency of the wax to a putty or liquid state. If you do not have an electric melter, simply cut a piece of wax with a hot blade, then place the wax in an ashtray or jar cover and, as you need it, melt it with the soldering iron to a putty or liquid consistency. You might also place the wax fragments in a tin can over which a light bulb is hung to keep the wax in a spreading consistency.

Apply the soft wax with your flat tool to add bulk or provide texture. Shape and smooth it with the heated tool as it cools. You will find that you are applying wax and

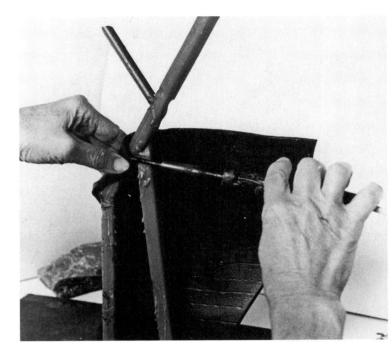

Fig. 8–7. Wherever the sheet forms touch one another or the rods they should be fused. Lightly melt the edge of the rod first, then touch heat to the sheet; remove heat and hold. (Photo by Lee Vold).

cutting wax away intermittently. You will also be welding form to form. As the knife is heating for some of these operations, you will be using the time to hold welded forms together while they cool and harden, or perhaps looking for an interesting scrap of wax to attach to a form and so on. Eventually, you will establish a rhythm between the various aspects of wax manipulation: heating, cutting, welding, holding, and soft wax application. Some of these operations are illustrated in figures 8–8 to 8–11.

Texture

The finished texture of the sculpture is an important consideration and may take many forms. It may be rough, swirled, or smooth; texture can also be made by imprinting the soft wax with objects and heavy fabrics.

For rough textures, melt fragments of wax to a putty consistency and apply the putty to your form in the desired texture. Note that if the surface form is cool, it should be heated slightly to permit good bonding of the soft wax. A rough texture can be dramatic, as it reflects light with its surface highlights and depressions. Since this can create the

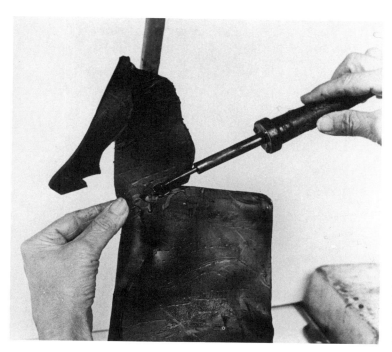

Fig. 8–8. Instead of pre-planning, proceed, in these first attempts, with a sense of experimentation: bravely apply and then cut, or cut and then apply your sheet wax patterns. (Photo by Lee Vold).

Fig. 8–9. Initially, you may apply too much heat and create holes in the wax, or too little heat and cause a wax section to drop off. Both conditions are easily rectified with reapplication of heat and wax. Hold joining edges for several seconds to create good adhesion. (Photo by Lee Vold).

Fig. 8–10. A form cut away from the sculpture often "goes" well in another area; that curve or angle, appearing elsewhere, also lends "visual logic" to the composition. (Photo by Lee Vold).

Fig. 8–11. When melting edges together, keep hands well out of the way of hot dripping wax. (Photo by Lee Vold).

illusion of depth, rough texturing might be particularly effective in a stylistically flat piece (figure 8–12).

For smooth textures, fold a piece of soft cotton material several times to form a pad. Moisten with a bit of light oil (mineral oil or machine oil). Touch the pad to the soldering iron or hot plate and rub it over the wax surface. (It will pick up wax and gradually become easier to use.) Smooth textures can enhance the lyrical quality of curved forms, as seen in portions of figure 8–1. In bronze, such forms are often polished and given a highly reflective patina (an expensive procedure).

For swirled textures, heat the wax tool and use the flat blade to lightly soften the wax surface. Move the tool across the form to create a random pattern of swirls (figure 8–13).

Drapery

Soft cotton material can be dipped in molten wax and applied to the sculpture to form drapery. The folds should be allowed to drape naturally (unless, of course, other spe-

Fig. 8–12. Rough texture can create the illusion of depth and might be particularly effective in a stylistically flat piece. [Judith Peck, *Figure 3;* (1976), Bronze, 19″ × 23″ (wall piece). (Photo by Jules Pinsley).]

Fig. 8–13. The texture of this piece is decoratively swirled. [Judith Peck, *Rooftop Sunbather*; (1976), Bronze, 8″ high, 12″ × 8¾″ at base. Collection, Myrtle Rosen. (Photo by Jules Pinsley).]

cific forms are intended). Reinforce thin portions of the drape by adding wax with the tool. Figure 8–14 illustrates drapery done in this manner. Drapery can also be created by fusing interesting shapes directly onto the form (figure 8–15).

FINISHING

Wax, as stated previously, is frequently cast in bronze (sources for bronze casting are included in the *References* section). Bronze casting is the most beautiful and lasting method of finishing but it is also the most expensive. Other methods are less successful as measured against bronze but are less costly. Moreover, it may take some time before mastery of the methods and materials of forming sculptures in

Fig. 8–14. Soft cotton material, dipped in molten wax, can be applied to the figure to form the basic structure of drapery. It is then reinforced and shaped with soft wax. [Judith Peck, *Music*; (1983), Bronze, 16″ high, 13″ × 9½″ at base. (Photo by Lee Vold).]

155

Fig. 8–15. Drapery can also be created by welding prepared shapes directly onto the form. [Judith Peck, *Flamenco;* (1965), Bronze edition (5), 12¾″ high, 6″ × 5½″ at base. Collection, Dr. Howard Goldstein, Dr. Laurie Bleicher, Louis Kramer, Sarah and Daniel Wofford. (Photo by Jules Pinsley).]

wax will result in a piece that is ready for casting. Therefore, laminating might be considered as a method for preserving wax. The challenge in laminating, whichever product or method is applied, is to avoid build-ups that will make the underlying forms cumbersome or unclear.

Lamination with Resin or Autobody Filler

Polyester or epoxy resin or autobody filler (see pages 37 and 58) can be applied directly to the wax form. Avoid drips and use a well-made brush to apply, as falling bristles are a nuisance. Use protective gloves and work in an area with excellent ventilation. If you propose to work any longer than half an hour or so with polyester or epoxy resin, you must purchase and use a respirator (a nose and mouth mask designed to eliminate organic vapors).

Lamination with Fiberglass and Resin

If lamination with fiberglass is to be the finishing method, the texture of the wax should be relatively smooth. Single strips of fiberglass coated with polyester resin are applied to the surface forms. The strips should be narrow and not too long so that the contours can be controlled and the forms do not become bulky. A single layer of fiberglass is sufficient. Rolls of fiberglass in varying widths from 1 inch to 12 inches, can be purchased; the rolls will not ravel to the extent that bolts of fiberglass will when cut.

When the resins have completely dried (overnight) and the surface is hard, the rough edges can be filed smooth with a metal rasp. The safety precautions above must be strictly observed when working with the resins in both their liquid (applying) and solid (filing) states.

Lamination with Sculpmetal or Model-Metal

Sculpmetal and Model-Metal (trade names) are products that combine aluminum powder and plastic resin. The product is thick enough to be used with a putty knife to create texture, or it can be thinned down with its accompanying solvent and applied with a brush.

Lamination with Pariscraft

For a description of Pariscraft, refer to chapter 3. Again, as in lamination with fiberglass, the wax surface should be fairly smooth so as not to distort your sculpture's line and form with the added layer of material.

Fig. 8–16. Abstract student sculpture in wax, laminated with autobody filler. Karen Sherman. (Photo by Lee Vold).

Strips of Pariscraft are cut, dipped in water, and applied to the wax by wrapping each strip closely around the form. Narrow strips are more easily controlled; therefore, it is a good idea to cut the strips lengthwise before applying.

Mounting

Select a base of appropriate dimensions, as described in chapter 9. The base, as in all mounting procedures, should be fully prepared—that is, sanded, then painted, stained, or burned. To remove the sculpture from your working base (which by now will be wax-encrusted), simply heat your flat blade and pass it under the form.

Mount your sculpture by melting a small amount of wax to the finished base in various places; then spot melt your sculpture to it. The laminating resin can be used as an adhesive as well. Take care that the mounting material (wax

Fig. 8–17. *Condor.* [Student sculpture in wax. Peter Nirchio. (Photo by Unhjem/ Cavallo).]

Fig. 8–18. *Flower Form.* [Student sculpture in wax. Stephen Issler. (Photo by Unhjem/Cavallo).]

drippings or resin) is not seen. If drippings should appear, scrape them off and retouch the base. In mounting, neatness counts.

Student sculptures in wax are illustrated in figures 8–17 to 8–19.

EXTENDING THE PROJECT: ART IN HUMAN SERVICE

Wax in thin fragments is pliable in the warmth of one's hands yet hardens when cool; moreover, for simple modeling procedures, one might manage with no tools. It is therefore an excellent semipermanent sculptural medium for use in institutional or agency settings where budgets, set-up time and space, and manual dexterity may be limited.

Imagery that may be particularly stimulating for self-expression and for promoting group discussion include: faces,

Fig. 8–19. Untitled student sculpture in progress. (Photo by Unhjem/Cavallo).

bodies, food, vehicles, animals, flowers, furniture, furnishings, and other artifacts from the real and natural world.

If hands alone are not sufficient for making the wax pliable, wax fragments can be placed in a bowl of hot water before modeling. Participants new to modeling in any medium are often self-conscious about "dirty" hands; therefore, be sure to have green soap and a nail or scrub brush available for clean-up.

Mounting and Finishing 9

MOUNTING serves not only to support the sculpture but to separate it from other objects in the surrounding area and give it its own immediate, custom-made environment. A sculpture is ready for presentation when positioned at a good height and location and lit so that its highlights and shadows are revealed to advantage.

In this chapter, guidelines are offered for mounting most of the sculptural media described in the book. Procedures particular to each project have also been provided at the end of each chapter.

THE APPROACH TO MOUNTING SCULPTURE

Just as you continually selected and judged relationships between forms and shapes during the evolution of your sculpture, you must now establish a relationship between sculpture and base by means of the same critical judgment.

It is important to keep in mind that the larger the base, the smaller your sculpture may appear. The more elaborate the base, the more diminished the sculpture may be in contrast. The idea is to enhance the sculpture, not the base; to show off the sculpture, not compete with it. So think in those terms when deciding what material to use as a base and what finish to apply. Then, carefully evaluate how the sculpture is to stand (stance); and what width, length, and thickness (size) of base is most desirable.

Choosing the Materials and the Finish

The choice of what material to use as a base and how to finish it will ultimately depend on the sculpture itself in each specific instance. Wooden bases are the most practical. They can be painted, waxed, oiled, varnished, laminated, or charred to a dark brown with a propane torch. Other suitable materials for bases are Plexiglas, concrete, slate, and various kinds of marble.

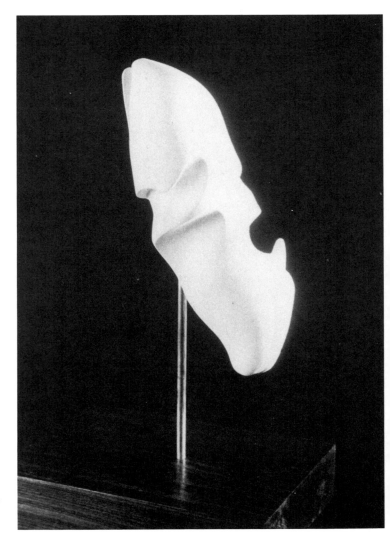

Fig. 9–1. A plaster carving mounted on an exposed stainless steel rod. [John Reda (student). (Photo by Unhjem/ Cavallo).]

The Stance of the Sculpture

If the sculpture is representational, it will no doubt have a defined presentation position. If abstract, it will also, in most cases, be conceived as standing in a particular way. But the fact that the sculpture physically balances in one position as it is being created does not mean that it has to be mounted that way. It may be dramatic, for example, tilted on end (figure 9–2), or mounted horizontally instead of vertically (figure 9–3). It may, if it is carved all around and does not have a flat bottom, work best mounted off the base with a portion of steel rod exposed (figures 9–4 and 9–5; see also figure 9–1).

A sculpture conceived one way, if worked on all sides, may present itself differently to you as you work it, and an alternate mounting may be preferable. Figures 9–6 and 9–7 show an abstract plaster form in two different positions. This requires a thoughtful choice by the artist as to which presentation is more dynamic.

There are many ways to prop the sculpture as you explore these various positions. Use pieces of wood, sandbags, or rocks as props—anything that will allow you to step back and make a well-thought-out decision. Finally, if one way seems to work particularly well, meaning that (a) you like it; (b) it has good internal dynamics in balance, tension, and rhythm; and (c) there seems to be a good relationship between sculptural forms and base, go with it.

Selecting the Size of the Base

Once you have determined the stance of the sculpture, the size of the supporting base—its width, length, and thickness—comes next. One way to determine size is to place your piece on a sheet of black construction paper near the corner edge of a table so that you can see it from the front and side (figure 9–8). Fold back or extend the paper on the sides and front to visualize different *widths and lengths* of base. Next, let the paper extend below the table a few inches; then fold it under or extend it to visualize how different *thicknesses* of dark wood will look. See how these varying sizes enhance or detract from your sculpture. The base should be neither too big nor too thick as this will dwarf the sculpture; on the other hand, it should not appear visually or structurally inadequate.

Considerations in Judging Base Width and Length

Generally speaking, and only as a very broad guideline to indicate how little base need show beneath the sculpture, about ½-inch beyond the sculpture on each side is a sufficient amount of base (figure 9–9). Your sculpture, however, may not have a baseline that lends itself to measurement; moreover, it may not be a central mass but may protrude markedly

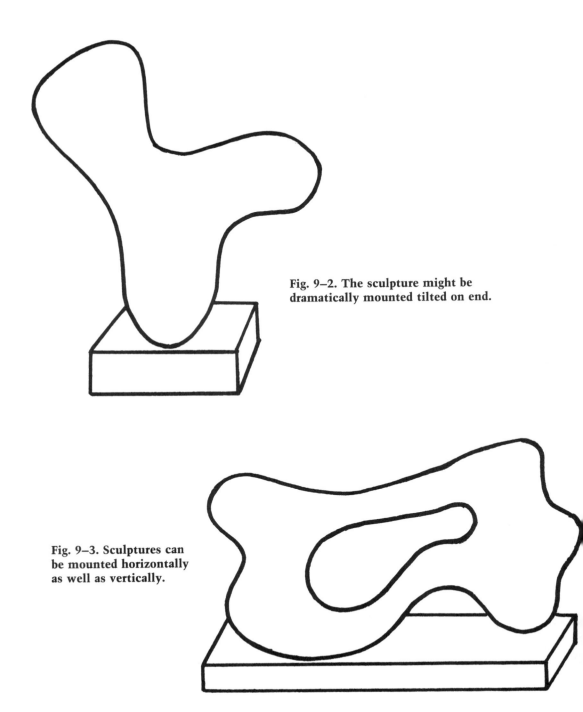

Fig. 9–2. The sculpture might be dramatically mounted tilted on end.

Fig. 9–3. Sculptures can be mounted horizontally as well as vertically.

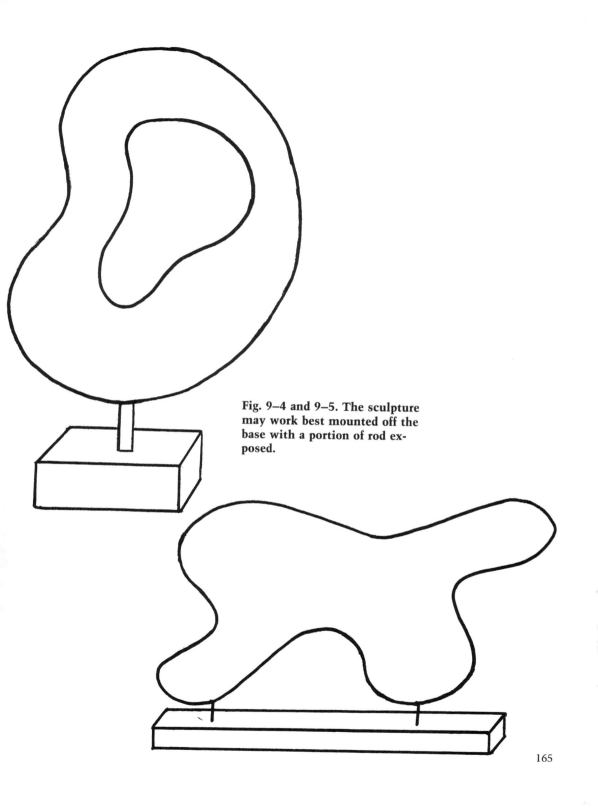

Fig. 9–4 and 9–5. The sculpture may work best mounted off the base with a portion of rod exposed.

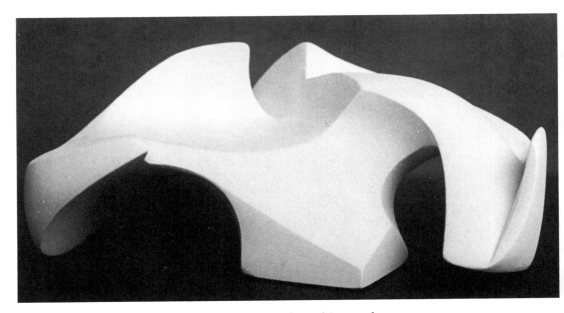

Figs. 9–6 and 9–7. The same sculpture held upright and inverted presents two very different choices in mounting. [John Reda (student). (Photo by Lee Vold).]

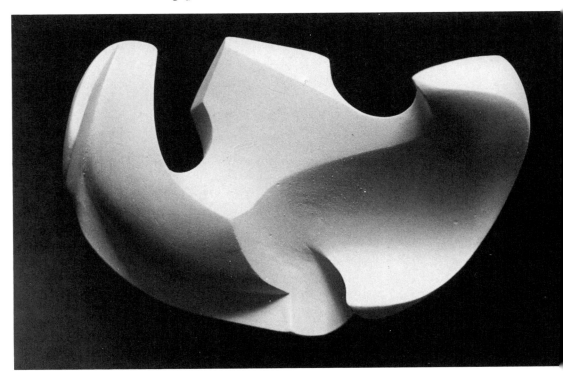

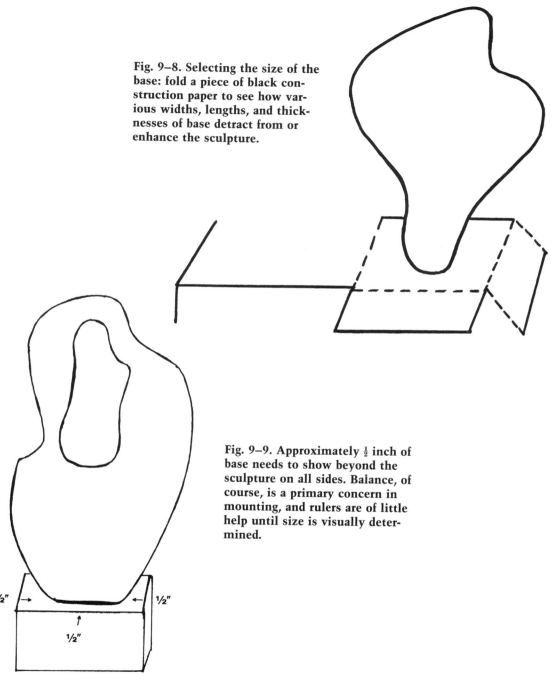

Fig. 9–8. Selecting the size of the base: fold a piece of black construction paper to see how various widths, lengths, and thicknesses of base detract from or enhance the sculpture.

Fig. 9–9. Approximately ½ inch of base needs to show beyond the sculpture on all sides. Balance, of course, is a primary concern in mounting, and rulers are of little help until size is visually determined.

½″

½″

½″

in one or more directions. You must visually assess all of these projections in balancing the sculpture on the base.

You may determine that the piece should overhang the base. This can be very effective, but be sure that the overhang visually balances with other forms on all sides (see figure 6–14).

Considerations in Judging Base Thickness

The size, delicateness, massiveness, or linear qualities of the sculpture may demand a thin base ($\frac{1}{2}$ inch to 1 inch), a thick base, or a cube. The thickness will vary, depending on all of these factors, but certain general considerations can be kept in mind:

- It is usually not aesthetically interesting to duplicate thicknesses. For example, if the sculpture is predominantly one or two thicknesses in its walls or height or width, the base should not be the same (figure 9–10).
- A thick base, as in figure 9–11, would probably be too massive for a slender sculptural form and tend to overwhelm it.
- A thin base, as in figure 9–12, might appear flimsy and inadequate for a sculpture with large forms.
- A square or rectangular form such as a head might be enhanced by a cube-shaped base (figure 9–13) or a base of equal surface size in width and length.

CHECKLIST OF TOOLS AND MATERIALS FOR WOODEN BASES

Not all of the items listed below (and shown in figure 9–14) are necessary for mounting any given sculpture. The checklist is inclusive so that you can scan it and prepare for what you might need. Your own sculpture will be unique, and you will have to make a decision in each instance as to which specific materials and method of mounting to use.

- Black construction paper: used to determine base size.
- Wood for bases: kiln-dried hardwood, plywood or chipboard.
- Rocks, sandbags, wooden sticks: to prop sculpture to determine stance (not shown).
- Ruler and pencil: for making accurate measurements before cutting.

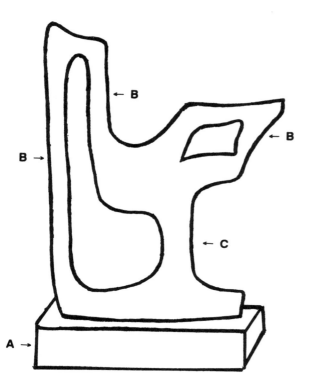

Fig. 9–10. Try not to duplicate the predominant thicknesses of the sculpture in the base. Here, the thickness of the base (A) is different from the predominant thicknesses of the sculpture walls (B and C).

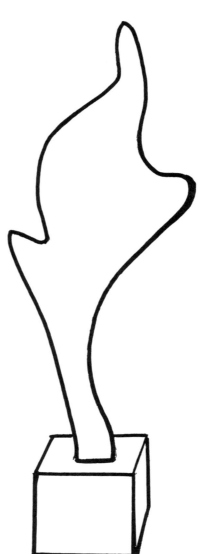

Fig. 9–11. A thick base might prove overwhelming for a slender sculptural form.

169

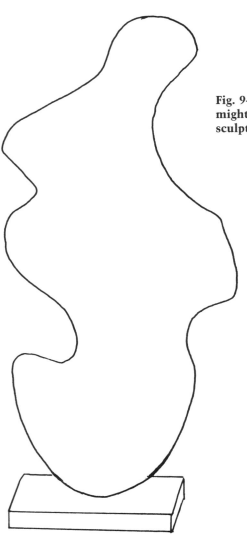

Fig. 9–12. A thin base
might appear flimsy for a
sculpture with large forms.

Fig. 9–13. A cube base
might be a good choice for a
square or rectangular form
such as a head.

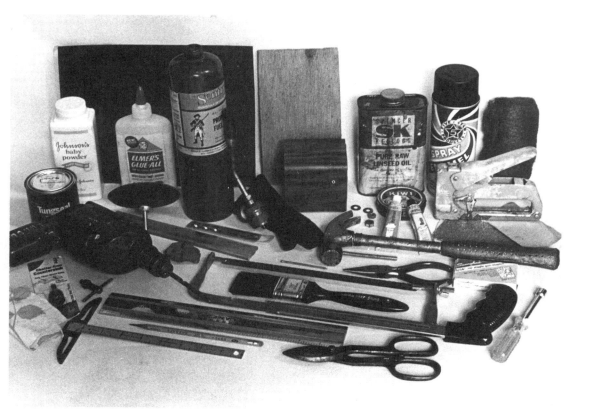

Fig. 9–14. Tools and materials for mounting on wooden bases. (Photo by Lee Vold).

- T square: for accurate squaring of bases.
- Saw: for cutting bases to size.
- Sandpaper: for smoothing bases.
- Kiwi shoe paste wax (dark brown and neutral): for finishing wooden base.
- Propane torch: for finishing wooden base by charring to a dark brown color.
- Steel wool: for cleaning wood after burning.
- Linseed oil: rubbed over charred wood or used alone as a final finish.
- Black spray enamel—flat, satin, or gloss: for finishing base.
- Varnish: for finishing base.

- Rags and brush: for applying wax, linseed oil, or varnish.
- $\frac{1}{4}$-inch or $\frac{3}{8}$-inch drill with $\frac{1}{4}$-inch steel bits: for boring holes to mount sculptures.
- Sanding attachment for drill: for sanding base.
- $\frac{1}{4}''$ masonry bit: for mounting plaster and cement and vermiculite sculptures.
- $\frac{1}{4}$-inch threaded steel rod with nuts and washers: for connecting sculpture to base.
- $\frac{3}{4}$-inch counter sink bit: drilled on reverse side of base to enable washer and nut to be affixed.
- Long-nosed pliers or nut-driver: for tightening nuts.
- Plastiline (oil-base clay): for aligning holes between sculpture and base.
- Talcum powder: used with plastiline for aligning holes.
- Five-Minute Epoxy resin and hardener: for adhering sculpture directly to base (hollow fired clay, found objects, wire) and for cementing rods into drilled holes.
- Hammer and nails: for mounting foil figures, found objects, wire sculptures.
- Staple gun and staples: for mounting foil figures, found objects, wire.
- White glue: for adhering felt to bottom of base.
- Felt—brown or black: glued to bottom of base to cover drill holes and protect furniture.

PROCEDURES FOR CONSTRUCTING A WOODEN BASE

Let us assume you are using a simple, flat wooden base. You can use plywood or chipboard if the base is to be painted and wood grain is not a factor, but use kiln-dried hardwood if the base is to be waxed, stained, or burned.

1. Measure the base with a pencil and T square to the proper dimensions.
2. Cut the base precisely so that if it is meant to be a square, it *is* square and if it is to be a rectangle, it *is* a rectangle. Take care not to splinter the wood at the end of the cut.
3. Sand the surface and edges of the wood.
4. Clean dust and debris from all surfaces.

Finishing the Wooden Base

The wooden base can be finished in a number of ways, depending on the color and texture desired and the kind of wood that is used. Below are some alternatives:

- Waxing, using dark brown Kiwi shoe polish in paste form; produces a handsome, lightly shiny finish with grain visible. Apply with a rag.
- Varnishing and wiping down; produces a glossy finish with grain visible.
- Burning with a propane torch; produces a brownish-black finish (depending on wood) with grain visible. Burning eliminates one step in base preparation, as sanding is not required. Work on a nonflammable surface such as a metal-topped table. Sweep the flame over all surfaces of the wood so that it chars evenly. Clean excess char with steel wool, then wipe the charred wood with a rag dipped in linseed oil.
- Spraying with black flat, semigloss, or gloss enamel; produces an opaque black finish with no grain visible. Before beginning, protect the surrounding area against overspray and support the base off the ground with a board so that the edges will coat and dry evenly. Follow the directions on the can for obtaining a smooth application.
- Laminate with Micarta or Formica (trade names); produces a semigloss or gloss sheet finish. Chipboard can be used as the base. Consult dealer for proper materials to use for adhesion. This is a more elaborate method, requiring other tools and materials than those listed and illustrated.

ATTACHING THE SCULPTURE TO THE BASE

Adhesion, for the purposes of the projects described in this text, will involve nailing, stapling, gluing, or drilling, sometimes in combination. Drilling holes and inserting threaded steel rods of appropriate proportion, fastened by nuts, will usually give the sculpture the stability it requires. However, if the work has been fired, it will be hollow, and there may be insufficient solid areas through which to drill. In that case, gluing may be a better choice. Many of the objects used in found-object sculpture may also lend themselves to gluing rather than drilling. The procedures offered in this section will have to be adapted to the specific requirements of your sculpture.

Procedures for Gluing

1. Place the sculpture on a level surface and locate two or three reasonably well-balanced points where the sculpture makes solid contact. Mark these spots on the bottom of the sculpture with a pencil.
2. Carefully position the sculpture on the base where you want it. You may want to tape cardboard onto the base temporarily if it can be marred easily. (If you do this, mark the sculpture's form on the cardboard.)
3. Place small wads of plastiline on the bottom of the sculpture at each of the pencil marks; then press the sculpture down at the appropriate place on the base. The clay will adhere to the cardboard or base, or at the very least, leave a stain. Before removing the cardboard, tap a small nail in and out to mark the spots.
4. Scratch the area of the base to be glued with steel wool or sandpaper so that the surface wax, paint, oil, or varnish is roughened sufficiently to allow for good adhesion.
5. Thoroughly mix equal parts of Five-Minute Epoxy resin and hardener with a nail on a piece of cardboard. Then, carefully bond the sculpture to the base, making sure that no glue oozes out, which would make the bond unsightly.
6. When dry, cut a piece of felt to size and glue it with white glue diluted slightly with water to the bottom of the sculpture to prevent marring of the furniture.

Drilling the Sculpture and Base

The procedures given are for moderate-size table sculptures or relatively lightweight wall reliefs. Begin as above by determining the stance of the sculpture on the base and selecting the point or points of contact.

1. Turn the sculpture upside-down by supporting it with sandbags and rocks. If the piece is cumbersome, set it in a trash can that has been filled with paper or rags for support (figure 9–15).

2. Place a drill bit on your drill. (Diameters will obviously need to be increased for heavy or massive sculptures.)

3. Determine the correct drilling angle according to the particular tilt, if any, the sculpture is expected to have on the base. If it is to be perfectly upright, the drilling angle will be perpendicular to the base or surface of the trash can (figure 9–15).

4. Drill as deeply as necessary to support the sculpture. If the sculpture is to be mounted flush to the base (not off the base with rod exposed), it will need more than one mounting point to prevent turning.

5. Cut a $\frac{1}{4}$-inch threaded steel rod to the depth of the hole you have drilled, adding to your measurement the thickness of your base (minus about $\frac{1}{4}$ inch). It is wise to affix the washer and nut on the rod before cutting, as the threads may become ragged after cutting. Put the rod aside.

6. Carefully set the sculpture on the base and determine precisely where you want it. When it is in place, tap the sculpture with your hand. A small puddle of material left in the holes from drilling will appear on the base, indicating the precise points for drilling. If there is no puddle of material remaining, put small wads of plastiline on the base in the approximate locations of the intended drilling points; dust with talc to prevent sticking; then position the sculpture on the base and press hard. The talc-covered clay will be marked with an imprint of the holes in the sculpture, indicating where the holes in the base should be drilled.

7. Drill the holes in the base. Attach a countersink bit on the drill (approximately $\frac{3}{4}$ inch diameter should do) and drill the reverse side of the base sufficiently to allow a washer and bolt to be affixed to the rod with no hardware extending beyond the bottom of the wood.

8. Invert the sculpture again; temporarily insert the threaded rod and place the base on top to make sure everything fits. If there is excess rod, cut it off or drill slightly deeper into the sculpture. (Before cutting the rod, be certain that the nut is already threaded on or can be threaded on easily.) Remove the rod.

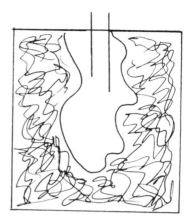

Fig. 9–15. Drilling the sculpture: turn the sculpture upside down in a trashcan filled with paper or rags. If the piece is to be perfectly upright, the drilling angle will be perpendicular to the base. More than one mounting point will be needed for good support and to prevent turning.

9. Mix equal parts of epoxy resin and hardener and bond the rod into the sculpture. Repeat the process for each rod. If the rods are to be glued into a hollow form—the modeled head in clay, for example—extra support is provided by coating a slender strip of fiberglass (or other cloth) with epoxy resin and bonding the rods to the inner walls with the resin-coated fabric. Use plastic gloves to avoid skin contact. Resins must never be touched with bare fingers or hands. If skin does contact epoxy resin, wash immediately with warm water and soap.

10. Slip the base onto the rods before setting occurs to make sure they remain in position, but do not proceed further until the epoxy sets.

11. Add the washer and nut and tighten.

12. Cut a piece of felt to size and attach it to the bottom with diluted white glue.

Professional Mounting for Difficult Pieces

As you progress, some of your sculptures may be of such stature and complexity that you want them mounted in a more sophisticated way than you can manage by yourself. That is, your accomplishment in creating sculpture may outdistance your skill in making bases. One of the sculpture services that is offered is professional mounting (see *References*). If there is a facility not too far away, you might consider bringing your piece to them. Competent carrpenters and cabinetmakers can also handle the task under your supervision.

PLACEMENT AND LIGHTING

Whether the finished sculpture is to be placed at eye level or above or below eye level is of consequence. For example, a lovely work placed too low may have little impact and become lost in a room. Sculpture will be seen in the manner in which it is displayed; that is, parts will be hidden from view at various heights and in various positions, and other aspects of the sculpture will be emphasized, largely according to placement. Experiment with placement just as you did in choosing a base and in all of the other formal decisions that you have been making right along.

Background is also of consequence. Your base was necessary not only to secure your piece but to set it off from its surroundings. Placement is also designed to set the sculpture off from its surroundings at the same time as it acts in concert with them. For example, high placement of a large sculpture might so unbalance other things in the room that although the piece itself might be majestic, adjacent furnishings might be dwarfed. Similarly, a grandiose, highly decorated object close to your sculpture might compete with the eloquent forms you had so carefully established. Competing colors and textures and other such conflicts should also be considered.

Simple pedestals enhance sculpture; they can be made of wood and painted or laminated in black Micarta or Formica. It is sometimes necessary to weight the base of the pedestal with lead to increase its sturdiness. (See *Sources of Supply* for pedestal manufacturers.)

Finally, the sculpture must have appropriate light. Lighting need not be elaborate, but it must be sufficient. Both daytime and nighttime illumination must be considered. Sometimes unexpected effects can occur with a change in lighting, for example, when light strikes from behind to illuminate the contours of negative forms in the sculpture or from underneath to give the sculpture a dramatic, monumental quality.

The finishing, mounting, placement, and lighting of the sculpture should not overemphasize the importance of the work you have made but rather demonstrate what was stated in the very first chapter: that sculpture exists in space. It can be seen only in relationship to the space around it.

Sculpture is an integration of forms, and those forms must integrate with the base and the environment. Sculpture is not a daub of this and a splash of that but the substantial interrelationship of form, mass, line, and shape. Well-conceived, fabricated, finished, and mounted, sculpture is dynamic movement—a gesture, a statement, a monumental moment caught in time and in place.

Appendices

SUPPLIES are listed in alphabetical order with the *type* of store or supplier where the material can be found. The list is followed by the names and addresses of specialized suppliers.

SOURCES OF SUPPLY

armatures and armature wire	sculpture supply
auto body filler	auto body shops
Carborundum papers	sculpture supply; hardware
cement (Portland)	lumber yards
chisels	sculpture supply; hardware
clay and clay tools	clay companies; sculpture, ceramic, and art supply
epoxy resin (Five-minute Epoxy), quick-setting (sold in twin tubes—resin and hardener) for bonding, liquid for laminating	plastics and marine supply
fiberglass (yardage or rolls)	plastics and marine supply
files and rasps	sculpture and art supply; hardware
Five-minute Epoxy	see epoxy
Flecto Varethane (plastic spray)	hardware
foil	household
gloves (plastic)	household; hardware
kilns	ceramic supply
knives	household; hardware
mallets	sculpture supply
masks (dust or respirator)	sculpture supply; industrial paint supply
mixing bowls	household
Pariscraft	arts and crafts supply
pedestals	sculpture services; furniture stores
plaster	hardware; art and sculpture supply; paint supply; gypsum companies
plastics (fiberglass and resins)	plastics and marine supply
sand	lumber yards
sandbags (ready-made)	sculpture supply; canvas for sewing—fabric or camping stores

Sculpmetal	sculpture and art supply
vermiculite	garden nurseries
wax	foundry suppliers; wax and sculpture supply
wax tools	sculpture supply
wire and wire tools	hardware

Arts and Crafts Suppliers

Art Pack
  8106 N. Denver
  Portland, OR 97217
Arthur Brown and Bro., Inc.
  2 West 46th St.
  New York, NY 10036
Dick Blick Co.
  P.O. Box 1267
  Galesburg, IL 61402
Dick Blick Co. East
  P.O. Box 26
  Allentown, PA 18105
Dick Blick West
  P.O. Box 521
  Henderson, NV 89015
Flax's Artist Materials
  1699 Market St.
  San Francisco, CA 94103
Flax Co., Inc.
  1001 East Jefferson St.
  Phoenix, AZ 85034
Sam Flax, Inc.
  (Three locations)
  425 Park Ave
  New York, NY 10022

  1401 E. Colonial Dr.
  Orlando, FL 32803

  1460 Northside Dr.
  Atlanta, GA 30318

Flax, Inc.
  8801 Sepulveda Blvd.
  Los Angeles, CA 90024
J. L. Hammett Co.
  2393 Vauxhall Rd.
  Union, NJ 07083
Nasco Arts and Crafts
  901 Janesville Ave.
  Fort Atkinson, WI 53538

Pyramid Artists' Materials
P.O. Box 877
Urbana, IL 61801
Sax Arts and Crafts
P.O. Box 2002
Milwaukee, WI 53201

Bronze (Metallic) Powder Suppliers

U.S. Bronze Powders, Inc.
Route 202
Flemington, NJ 08822

Clay Suppliers (See also Arts and Crafts Suppliers)

A.R.T. Studio Clay Company
921 Oakton St.
Elk Grove Village, IL 60007
Sculptor's Supplies, Ltd.
220 E. 6th St.
New York, NY 10003

Perma-Flex Mold Co.
1919-T Livingston St.
Columbus, OH 43209
Sculpture House
38 East 30th St.
New York, NY 10016

Kiln Suppliers

A.R.T. Studio Clay Company
1555 Louis Ave.
Elk Grove Village, IL 60007
Ceramic Supply of New York and New Jersey
534 La Guardia Place
New York, NY 10012

10 Dell Glen Ave.
Lodi, NJ 07644

Paragon Industries (contact for local area distributors)
2202 E. Scyene Rd.
Mesquite, TX 75149

Plastics, Fiberglass, and Resin Suppliers

Berton Plastics, Inc.
170 Wesley Ave.
Hackensack, NJ 07601
Defender Industries, Inc.
P.O. Box 820
255 Main St.
New Rochelle, NY 10802

Industrial Plastics
324 Canal St.
New York, NY 10013

Sculpture Services (information, mounting, pedestals)

International Sculpture Center (publishes *Sculpture* and
sponsors conferences)
1050 Potomac St. NW.
Washington, DC 20007
Johnson Atelier (apprenticeships, casting, fabrication,
enlarging, technical services)
60 Ward Ave Extension
Mercerville, NJ 08619
Montoya Art Studios (casting, mounting, carving stones,
supplies)
435 Southern Blvd.
West Palm Beach, FL 33405
Sculpture House Casting (casting, mounting, pedestal
fabrication)
30 East 30th St.
New York, NY 10016
Sculpture Review (illustrated articles; ads for sculpture
services)
The National Sculpture Society
15 East 26 St.
New York, NY 10010

Sculpture Suppliers

Sculptor's Supplies, Ltd.
220 E. 6th St.
New York, NY 10003
Sculpture House
30 East 30th St.
New York, NY 10016
Flatlanders
11993 E. US-223
Blissfield, MI 49228
Montoya/MAS International, Inc.
435 Southern Blvd.
West Palm Beach, FL 33405

Wax Suppliers

M. Argueso and Co. (brown and black microcrystalline slabs)
441 Waverly Ave
Mamaroneck, NY 10543

Kindt-Collins Co. (sprue waxes, also called extrusion waxes—
many shapes and diameters). For types referred to in text,
order: $\frac{1}{2}$-inch square cored red #9; $\frac{1}{4}$-inch round solid green
#16; soft brown sculpture wax; $\frac{1}{8}$-inch wax sheets
12651 Elmwood Ave.
Cleveland, OH 44111
Premier Wax Co., Inc.
3327 Hidden Valley Dr.
Little Rock, AR 72212

REFERENCES AND RESOURCES

THE references and resources listed in this section are provided for readers who want to expand their creative work in
a method described or referred to in the text; to broaden
their knowledge of contemporary sculpture techniques and
productions; or to avail themselves of casting services. The
list is by no means complete and is intended only as an
introductory reference source.

Art in Human Service

American Art Therapy Association, Inc. (information,
publications, education, conferences)
505 E. Hawley St.
Mundelein, IL 60060
American Journal of Art Therapy
Vermont College of Norwich Univ.
Montpelier, VT 05602
Stern's Book Service (comprehensive mail-order service)
5806 N. Magnolia St.
Chicago, IL 60660

Bronze Sculpture Casting Foundries

Excalibur Bronze Foundry, Inc.
85 Adams St.
Brooklyn, NY 11201
House Bronze
6804 66th St.
Lubbock, TX 79409
Johnson Atelier
Ward Ave. Extension
Mercerville, NJ 08619
Joel Meisner Foundry
115 Schmitt Blvd.
Farmingdale, NY 11735

Mengel Art Foundry
    1975 Airport Industrial Park
    Marietta, GA. 30062
P.S.H. Industries, Inc. (laminating in sprayed metal)
    5346 East Ave.
    La Grange, IL 60525
Shidoni Foundry
    P.O. Box 250
    Tesuque, NM 87574
Morris Singer Foundry, Ltd.
    Bond Close, Basingstoke, Hants
    RG24 OPT.
    England

Carving—Methods (Wood and Stone)

Andrews, Oliver. *Living Materials.* Berkeley: U. of California
    Press, 1983.
Langland, Tuck. *Practical Sculpture.* Englewood Cliffs: Prentice-
    Hall, 1988.

Casting and Mold-making—Methods (see Plaster)

Cold Casting and Mold-making—Services

Sculpture House Casting
    30 E. 30th St.
    New York, NY 10016
Johnson Atelier
    Ward Ave. Extension
    Mercerville, NJ 08619
Rocca/Noto Studios, Inc.
    10-06 38th Ave.
    Long Island City, NY 11101

Clay—Methods

Padovano, Anthony. *The Process of Sculpture.* Garden City:
    Doubleday and Co., 1981.
Lucchesi, Bruno and Malmstrom, Margit. *Terra Cotta: The
    Technique of Fired Clay Sculpture.* New York: Watson-Guptil,
    1977.

Fiberglass (see Plastics)

Plaster—Methods

Chaney, Charles, and Skee, Stanley. *Plaster Mold and Model Making*. New York: Simon & Schuster, 1973.

Farnworth, Warren. *Creative Work with Plaster*. London & Sydney: B.T. Batsford Ltd., 1975.

Meilach, D.Z. *Creating with Plaster*. London: Blandford Press and U.S.A.: Reilly & Lee Co., 1968.

Wagner, Victor H. *Plaster Casting for the Student Sculptor*. London: Alec Tiranti, 1970.

Plastics—Methods

Newman, Thelma R. *Plastics as an Art Form*, revised edition. Philadelphia: Chilton Book Co., 1969

Padovano, Anthony. *The Process of Sculpture*. Garden City: Doubleday & Co., 1981.

Portrait Sculpture—Methods

Lucchesi, Bruno and Malmstrom, Margit. *Modeling the Head in Clay*. New York: Watson-Guptil, 1979.

Sand Casting—Method

Villiard, Paul. *The Art and Craft of Sand Casting*. New York: Funk & Wagnalls, 1975.

Welding—Methods

Irving, Donald. *Sculpture: Materials and Process*. New York: Simon & Schuster, 1970

Griffin, I.H., Roden, E.M., and Briggs, C.W. *Basic Oxyacetylene Welding*, 3rd ed. Albany: Delmar, 1977.

Wire—Methods

Brommer, Gerald F., *Wire Sculpture*. Worcester: Davis, 1968.

Padovano, Anthony. *The Process of Sculpture*. Garden City: Doubleday and Co., 1981.

Index

Page Numbers in *italic* indicate illustrations